PIE SHELL CREATIONS
from Pet-Ritz ®

If you have a weakness for plump fresh blueberries baked between layers of flaky pastry, or rich creamy cheesecake laced with bananas and spice, you've come to the right place. We've packed this book with all the old-time favorites, along with some up-and-coming specialties—there are fruit pies, cream pies, custard pies, flans, dumplings, tarts, cheesecakes, and ice cream pies. But we didn't stop with dessert pies. We've also included creative recipes for classic quiches, hearty meat pies, crusty casseroles, and flaky turnovers.

Pet-Ritz can show you how to make pies for any occasion using their convenient frozen pie crust shells. So turn the page for some scrumptious eating you won't soon forget—and it's all Pet-Ritz easy!

Pictured on the front and back cover: Chicken Pot Pie (recipe, page 46), Taco Pie (recipe, page 45), Cherry Peach Pie (recipe, page 74), Tuna Turnovers (recipes, page 55), and Strawberry Cheesecake Pie (recipe, page 92).

Better Homes and Gardens
TEST KITCHEN ®

This seal assures you that every recipe in Pie Shell Creations from Pet-Ritz is tested and approved by the Better Homes and Gardens® Test Kitchen. Each recipe is tested for family appeal, practicality, and deliciousness.

Produced by Meredith Publishing Services, 1716 Locust St., Des Moines, Iowa 50336.

contents

1

Pie crust cooking
made Pet-Ritz easy

2

Light lunches
quick as quiche

3

Enticing entrées
under a crust

4

Pies and pastries
for a perfect ending

5

Dazzling desserts
to dwell on

Pie crust cooking made Pet-Ritz easy

We'd like you to meet the "family" of *Pet-Ritz®* frozen pie crust shells. You'll find each member of the trio is designed to satisfy a unique cooking need—and to make your job in the kitchen easier. First of all, we'll introduce you to cooking with Pet-Ritz Pie Crust Shells in this opening chapter. Then, we'll capture your interest and whet your appetite with dozens of photographs and over 160 recipes for both main dishes and desserts. Now, we'd like to tell you about the Pet-Ritz family:

Pet-Ritz Regular 9-inch Pie Crust Shells are available in two package sizes: 10-ounce size, containing two crusts per package; and the 25-ounce size, containing five crusts per package. One Pet-Ritz Regular Pie Crust Shell will hold approximately 2⅔ cups filling.

Pet-Ritz "Deep Dish" 9-inch Pie Crust Shells are available in a 12-ounce package, containing two crusts per package. One Pet-Ritz Deep Dish Pie Crust Shell will hold approximately 4 cups filling.

Pet-Ritz 9-inch Graham Cracker Crusts are available in a 10-ounce package, containing two crusts per package. One Pet-Ritz Graham Cracker Crust will hold approximately 2⅔ cups of filling.

Pull a Pet-Ritz Graham Cracker Crust from the freezer and you can put together Frozen Yogurt Pie in just 10 minutes. The instructions for the frosting mix fix-up filling are on page 84.

Get the morning off to a good start with Egg and Sausage Quiche baked in Pet-Ritz Regular Pie Crust Shell. The recipe is on page 24.

Two Pet-Ritz "Deep Dish" Pie Crust Shells sandwich the spiced meat and fruit filling in Pork and Apple Pie. Look for this hearty recipe on page 39.

Perfect Single Crust Pie

Serving delicious cream pies, fluffy chiffons, or warm-from-the-oven custards is twice the fun and half the hassle when you start with *Pet-Ritz* frozen Pie Crust Shells.

Step by step

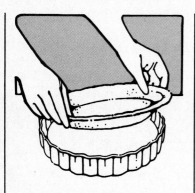

Here's how to transfer frozen pie crusts from the aluminum pie pan they come in to your own pie plates and baking dishes:

1. Remove the pie shell from the freezer. Run a knife between the crimped edge and aluminum foil pan to loosen the frozen crust. NOTE: Transferring shell should only be attempted while crust is FROZEN.

2. Place the FROZEN pie shell in a glass or ceramic pie plate. As pie shell begins to thaw, it will conform to the shape of the pie plate. This will take about 10 to 20 minutes, depending on the temperature of the room.

3. With your fingers, gently press the crust to fit your pan. Press and stretch the pastry so that the crimped edge lies on the rim of the pie plate.

4. Recrimp edge of crust. Proceed as directed in specific recipe.
   Regular size Pet-Ritz *Pie Crust Shells* fit baking dishes or pans 8 inches or less in diameter.
   "Deep Dish" Pet-Ritz *Pie Crust Shells* fit baking dishes or pans 9 to 10 inches in diameter.

To bake empty pie crust shell:

1. Remove frozen pie crust from freezer and let thaw at room temperature for 10 minutes.

2. Place a cookie sheet on rack near center of oven. Preheat oven to 400°.

3. Prick bottom and sides of thawed pastry with tines of fork so that the crust will not bubble up as pastry bakes.

4. Place pie pan on preheated cookie sheet. Bake 10 minutes or until lightly browned. If pie shell puffs during baking, remove shell from oven; prick again and return to oven.

5. Remove baked pie shell from oven and place on wire rack to cool completely.

6. Fill with desired filling.

To prebake shell for one crust pie:

1. Place a cookie sheet on rack near center of oven. Preheat oven to 450°.

2. Remove frozen pie crust from freezer. *Do not prick.* Place on preheated cookie sheet. Bake 6 minutes.

3. Remove pie crust from oven. Reduce oven temperature according to recipe directions.

4. While crust is prebaking, prepare filling. (If filling takes longer than 10 minutes to prepare, do this step first.)

5. Pour prepared filling into partially baked crust. Return to oven and bake on cookie sheet according to recipe directions.

6. To check for doneness, insert knife in filling just off center. If knife comes out clean, remove pie from oven and place on wire rack to cool completely. If filling clings to knife, continue baking until filling is set and pie tests done.

Coconut Cream Pie (pictured above)

1 *Pet-Ritz* "Deep Dish" Pie
  Crust Shell
1 cup sugar
½ cup all-purpose flour *or* ¼ cup
  cornstarch
¼ teaspoon salt
3 cups milk
4 egg yolks
3 tablespoons butter *or*
  margarine
1½ teaspoons vanilla
1 can (3½-ounce) flaked coconut
  (about 1⅓ cups)
4 egg whites
1 teaspoon vanilla
½ teaspoon cream of tartar
½ cup sugar

If desired, transfer frozen pie shell to glass or ceramic pie plate, according to directions on page 6. Thaw pie crust 10 minutes. Prick bottom and sides thoroughly with tines of fork. Bake in a 400° oven for 10 minutes. Remove pie crust from oven; cool.

In saucepan combine 1 cup sugar, flour or cornstarch, and salt. Stir in milk. Cook and stir until mixture thickens and bubbles. Reduce heat; cook and stir 2 minutes more. Remove pan from heat. Beat yolks slightly. Gradually stir *1 cup* of the hot mixture into yolks. Return to mixture in saucepan; cook and stir 2 minutes more. Remove from heat. Stir in butter and vanilla. Stir in *1 cup* of the coconut. Pour mixture into baked pie shell. In mixer bowl beat egg whites, vanilla, and cream of tartar until soft peaks form (tips curl over). Gradually add sugar, beating until stiff peaks form (tips stand straight). Spread meringue over hot filling, sealing to edge. Sprinkle with shredded coconut, if desired. Bake in 350° oven until meringue is golden, 12 to 15 minutes. Cool.

Double Crust Pies

Enclose a sweet fruit filling, in a tender delicate pastry, and you've captured the freshness and flavor that's become America's favorite dessert. (Of course, you can make it even better by teaming up that piece of pie with a generous scoop of vanilla ice cream.) Or, you can sandwich a hearty meat, fish, or poultry mixture between two golden crusts, and serve a plump and juicy main dish as easy as pie.

Either way, *Pet-Ritz* has the beginnings for your best-ever pie. And, you'll find plenty of recipes for both kinds of fillings on the following pages of this book. *Pet-Ritz* makes the pastry "packaging" simple with step-by-step instructions for using their frozen Regular or "Deep Dish" Pie Crust Shells. Follow along for fool-proof double crust pies.

Step by step

To assemble a double crust pie:

1. Remove the pie crust shells from the freezer. Invert one frozen crust onto waxed paper or package insert. Let crust thaw at room temperature until it flattens, about 10 to 15 minutes. (Allow second crust to stand at room temperature in aluminum pan.)

2. While crust is thawing on waxed paper, prepare the pie filling. (If filling takes longer than 15 minutes to prepare, prepare pie filling first.)

3. Pour filling into second crust in pie pan. Moisten edge of bottom crust with a little water so that top crust will adhere to it.

4. If a smooth top crust is desired, place thawed crust between two pieces of waxed paper and roll lightly with rolling pin just until evenly flattened.

5. Using waxed paper to lift and transfer pastry, invert flattened crust on top of filling; peel off paper.

6. Tuck the top crust edge under bottom crust edge and crimp by pinching between thumb and forefinger.

7. Cut several slits in top crust of pie to allow steam to escape during baking.

8. Place pie on preheated cookie sheet on rack near center of oven. Bake according to recipe directions. Remove pie from oven and place on wire rack to cool.

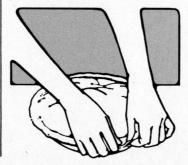

Add an attractive glaze to a double crust pie:

Sugar Glaze
Follow the directions for a double crust pie, but before baking, brush the top crust with a little milk, and sprinkle lightly with granulated sugar. The topping adds a rich brownness to fruit pies.

Cinnamon Sugar Glaze
Follow the directions for a double crust pie, but before baking, brush top crust with a little milk and sprinkle lightly with mixture of 2 tablespoons granulated sugar and ¼ teaspoon ground cinnamon. The glaze adds spice to oven-baked fruit pies.

Blueberry Pie (pictured above)

2 *Pet-Ritz* "Deep Dish" Pie
  Crust Shells
4 cups fresh blueberries
¾ to 1 cup sugar
3 tablespoons all-purpose flour
½ teaspoon finely shredded lemon
  peel
  Dash salt
1 to 2 teaspoons lemon juice
1 tablespoon butter *or* margarine
  Milk
  Sugar

Remove pie crust shells from freezer. Place one shell in glass or ceramic pie plate and let thaw 10 minutes. Fit pastry to bottom and sides of pie plate according to directions on page 6. Invert second crust onto waxed paper or insert and let thaw 10 to 15 minutes.

In mixing bowl combine blueberries, sugar, flour, lemon peel, and salt. Pour filling into crust in pie plate. Drizzle with lemon juice and dot with butter or margarine. Moisten edge of crust with a little water. Invert flattened crust on top of filling. Tuck edge under and crimp. Cut slits for escape of steam. Bake in 400° oven for 35 to 40 minutes. Brush top of pie with milk; sprinkle with additional sugar.

Lattice-top Double Crust Pie

Put the finishing touch on your favorite double crust pie with a fancy lattice crust. The elaborate look is easier than you'd guess. With the help of *Pet-Ritz* frozen Pie Crust Shells, you can turn a plain pie into something very special. Here's all the weaving instructions for the crust that you'll need to master the lattice technique.

Step by step

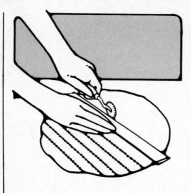

To make a lattice-top pie:

1. Remove frozen pie crust shells from freezer. Invert one crust onto waxed paper or waxed insert. Let crust thaw at room temperature until crust flattens, about 10 to 15 minutes.

2. While crust is thawing, prepare filling. (If filling takes longer than 15 minutes to prepare, do this step first.)

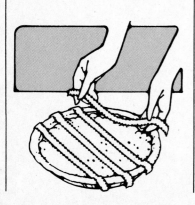

3. *To make lattice top, roll thawed crust lightly with rolling pin just until smooth and evenly flattened. Cut dough into ½- to ¾-inch-wide strips with a pastry wheel or sharp knife. (For a prettier top, use a ruler or straightedge to make uniform strips.)*

4. *Pour filling into second crust in pie pan.*

5. *Lay half of the cut strips of pie crust, parallel, on top of the filled pie, having strips spaced at one-inch intervals.*

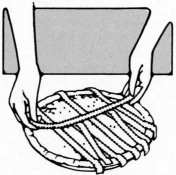

6. Working carefully, fold back every other strip already in place on top of filling. To begin weaving pastry strips, place one of the remaining pastry strips across center of pie at right angles to the first *half* of strips on the pie.

7. Gently unfold the folded pastry strips; fold back the strips that were straight. Add a second pastry strip parallel to the last, and at

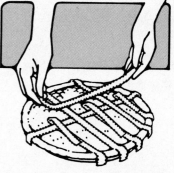

right angles to the folded strips. Leave a one-inch space between strips. Repeat this weaving process until the lattice top of the pie is complete.

8. Moisten edge of pie crust and crimp by pinching with thumb and forefinger sealing edge of bottom crust and ends of lattice strips.

9. Place on preheated cookie sheet on rack near center of oven. Bake according to recipe directions. Remove from oven and place on wire rack to cool.

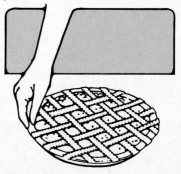

Cherry Raspberry Pie (pictured above)

2 *Pet-Ritz* "Deep Dish" Pie
   Crust Shells
1 package (10-ounce) frozen red
   raspberries, thawed
¾ cup sugar
3 tablespoons cornstarch
¼ teaspoon salt
2 cups pitted fresh tart red cherries *or* frozen tart red cherries, thawed and drained

Remove pie crusts from freezer. Invert one crust onto waxed paper and let thaw until flattened, about 10 to 15 minutes. Transfer second crust to glass or ceramic pie plate if desired, according to directions on page 6.

Drain raspberries; reserve syrup. Add water to syrup to make 1 cup. In saucepan mix sugar, cornstarch, and salt. Stir in reserved syrup and cherries. Cook and stir over medium-high heat until bubbly; cook and stir 1 minute more. Remove from heat; stir in raspberries. Cool 10 minutes. Pour filling into second crust in pie pan or plate. Top with lattice crust, according to directions on opposite page. Bake in 375° oven for 35 to 40 minutes. Cool on wire rack.

Graham Cracker Crusts

The texture and sweet, nutlike wheat flavor of graham cracker crust makes a delicious change from the traditional pastry pie crust. You'll find the taste of a *Pet-Ritz* Graham Cracker Crust will go well with fluffy chiffons, luscious cheesecake fillings, ice creams, and silken cream fillings. Since the crust is ready right from the freezer, graham cracker shells are ideal for no-bake fillings. And, they're just as versatile as a base for baked cheesecakes or meringue-topped cream pies. You'll want to keep some graham cracker pie crust shells on hand for a head-start on a scrumptious dessert.

Step by step

To make a cream-filled graham cracker crust pie:

1. Prepare filling.

2. Remove frozen graham cracker crusts from freezer. Open package and remove crusts.

3. Holding tabs on opposite sides of crusts, pull upward to break open protective plastic. Lift off plastic.

4. If only one pie shell is needed, replace second crust in plastic bag, seal and return to freezer.

5. Pour cream filling directly into graham cracker crust.

6. If desired, top hot filling with meringue. Spoon the meringue around edges first, spreading toward center. Seal meringue to edge of crust to prevent shrinkage of meringue during baking.

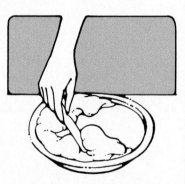

7. Place on preheated cookie sheet in 350° oven for 12 to 15 minutes, or until meringue is golden.

To make a baked graham cracker crust pie or cheesecake:

1–4. Repeat first four steps above.

5. Pour pie filling directly into frozen pie crust. Set on preheated cookie sheet on rack near center of oven and bake according to recipe directions.

6. To check for doneness at end of minimum time given in recipe, insert knife in filling just off center. If knife comes out clean, remove pie from oven and cool on wire rack. If filling clings to knife, continue baking until filling is set and pie tests done with a knife.

S'More Pie (pictured above)

- 2 cups milk
- 2 egg yolks
- 1 package (3⅛-ounce) *regular* vanilla pudding mix
- 1 cup tiny marshmallows
- 1 *Pet-Ritz* Graham Cracker Crust
- 2 milk chocolate candy bars (1.2-ounce each), broken in pieces
- 2 egg whites
- ½ teaspoon vanilla
- ¼ teaspoon cream of tartar
- ¼ cup sugar

Beat together milk and egg yolks just until blended. Gradually add milk-egg mixture to pudding mix in saucepan. Cook according to package directions. Remove from heat. Cover surface of pudding with waxed paper; cool. Sprinkle the marshmallows over the bottom of the graham cracker crust; top with the broken chocolate pieces. Spoon cooled pudding evenly over chocolate.

In small mixer bowl beat egg whites, vanilla, and cream of tartar at medium speed of electric mixer until soft peaks form, about 1 minute. Gradually add the sugar, beating at high speed until stiff peaks form (tips stand straight). Spread on top of pie, sealing to edges of crust. Bake in 350° oven for 12 to 15 minutes or until meringue is golden. Cool before serving.

Microwave Cooking

When time and energy (yours) are in short supply, microwave cooking and *Pet-Ritz* pie crusts make good teammates. The frozen pie crusts save you preparation steps; the microwave oven cuts cooking time.

 Although microwave cooking instructions will vary according to manufacturer, these general rules apply when using *Pet-Ritz* **frozen pie crust shells:**

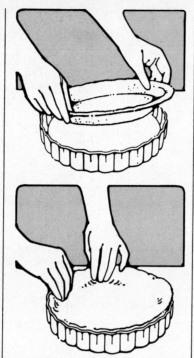

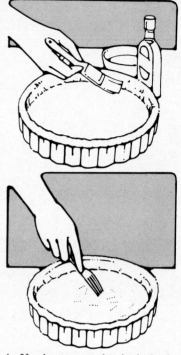

1. Remove pie shell from freezer. Run a knife between crimp and foil pan to loosen. NOTE: Transferring shell should only be attempted while FROZEN.
2. Place the FROZEN pie shell in glass or ceramic pie plate. As shell begins to thaw it will conform to the shape of the pie plate, about 10 to 20 minutes.
3. Gently press dough to bottom and sides of dish. Crimp edge.

4. If a browner color is desired, brush dessert pastries with vanilla flavoring; use Worcestershire sauce for meat pies.

5. For a baked empty crust, prick bottom and sides of shell with fork. For double-crust pie, fill shell, top with second crust, and crimp.

6. Cook according to manufacturer's microwave recipe.

Microwave Crab Meat Quiche

Use this recipe as a guide for creating your own microwave quiches—

1 *Pet-Ritz* "Deep Dish" Pie Crust Shell
1 cup (4 ounces) shredded Swiss cheese
1 can (7½ ounce) crab meat, drained, flaked, and cartilage removed
2 green onions, sliced
1½ cups light cream
½ teaspoon finely shredded lemon peel
¼ teaspoon dry mustard Dash ground mace
4 eggs
¼ cup sliced *Funsten* Almonds

Transfer crust to nonmetal pie plate according to directions above. Micro-cook *unpricked* crust at medium-high power for 8 to 12 minutes, giving a half turn after 4 minutes.

 Sprinkle cheese on bottom of crust. Top with crab and onion. In a 4-cup glass measure combine cream, ½ teaspoon *salt*, peel, mustard, and mace. Micro-cook on high power for 2 to 3 minutes or until boiling. Beat eggs; gradually stir in hot cream mixture. Pour over crab in crust. Top with almonds. Micro-cook on medium power 17 to 19 minutes, giving dish quarter turns every 5 minutes. Let stand 10 minutes. Makes 6 servings.

Keeping Pies Fresh

Proper pie storage is important to both flavor, freshness, and food safety. Use the following tips for keeping leftover pies at their best.

Cream pies

After cooling pies to room temperature, cover and refrigerate.

To cover a meringue-topped pie, insert several toothpicks halfway into the surface of the meringue. Loosely cover with clear plastic wrap allowing toothpicks to hold wrap away from meringue. Store in refrigerator.

Chiffon pies

Cool crust completely before filling. A warm crust will melt the chiffon mixture and decrease the volume of the filling.

To obtain a fluffy filling, chill chiffon mixture until it mounds slightly when spooned, then pile into pie shell. Chill until firm.

To prevent the surface of the chiffon from drying and becoming rubbery during prolonged storage, place the pie pan on a plate and cover with a large inverted mixing bowl.

Frozen Ice Cream Pies

Ice cream and other frozen pie fillings should be tightly covered during storage to prevent drying. Before serving, the pies should be allowed to stand at room temperature for 10 to 15 minutes. This "softening" time will make serving easier and improve the taste.

Custard Pies

Quiches are generally served hot, but any leftover wedges should not be allowed to set out at room temperature. Cover and refrigerate. If desired, reheat quiche in warm oven, or serve cold as an entrée or appetizer.

Sweet custard, pumpkin, and pecan pies contain eggs and/or milk, too. So be sure to store these pies in the refrigerator to prevent food spoilage.

Fruit Pies

Freshly baked pies should be placed on a wire rack and allowed to cool at room temperature. The rack allows air to circulate under the pie, preventing the pie from steaming and causing the crust to be soggy.

Fruit pies can be stored for a short time at room temperature, but they should be covered and refrigerated to retain freshness during prolonged storage.

To freeze a double crust fruit pie before baking, *do not* cut slits in top crust. Cover pie with inverted large paper plate to protect crust. Wrap in aluminum foil or moisture-vaporproof material; seal and label. If desired, place in a sturdy box or freezer container for additional protection. Freeze up to two months. To serve, unwrap pie and cut slits in top crust for escape of steam. Bake frozen pie in 450° oven for 15 minutes. Reduce temperature to 350°-375° and bake 45 to 50 minutes, or until done.

To freeze a double crust fruit pie after baking, cool the pie to room temperature on wire rack. (Be sure pie is cooled enough, or steam will form when pie is wrapped and placed in freezer.) Wrap cooled pie tightly with aluminum foil, label and freeze. To serve, thaw wrapped pie at room temperature 30 minutes.

Meat Pies

Freshly baked meat, fish, or poultry pies should be placed on a wire rack and allowed to stand at room temperature for 10 minutes. This allows the pie filling to set up and makes cutting and serving the pieces easier.

Any leftover pie should be covered and stored in the refrigerator. Reheat in a warm oven to serve.

Change-a-Crust

A little imagination can transform a plain pastry shell into a pièce de résistance pie. Try your hand at creating a special crust by adding a surprise lining to a cream-filled crust, or an enticing glaze on a double crust fruit or meat pie. You'll find some interesting ideas and techniques below.

Step by step

Try lining a pie shell with nuts, chocolate, or coconut.

Pecan Pie Crust

Follow the directions for baked pie shells on page 6, but before baking crust, sprinkle with 2 to 3 tablespoons chopped pecans. Press pecans gently into crust. Bake and fill. Next time use chopped walnuts or unsalted peanuts.

Coconut Pie Crust

Follow directions for baked pie shell on page 6, but before baking crust, sprinkle sides and bottom of crust with 3 to 4 tablespoons flaked coconut. Press coconut gently into crust. Bake and fill.

Chocolate Pie Crust

Follow directions for baked pie shells on page 6, but before baking, sprinkle pie shell with ⅓ cup semisweet chocolate chips. Bake as directed; remove pie crust from oven. Using back of spoon or knife, spread melted chocolate in thin layer over bottom and up the sides of the pie shell. Spoon cooled cream filling into pie shell.

Decorate double crust pies, turnovers, and dumplings with pastry cutouts.

Use small cookie cutters or the tip of a sharp knife, to cut out small leaf-shaped pastry designs. (Or, try your hand at creating your own imaginative shapes.) Brush the top of the unbaked pie, turnover, or dumpling with a mixture of 1 slightly beaten egg and 1 tablespoon water, so cutout will adhere to crust. Arrange pastry cutouts in decorative design on top of crust. Brush again with egg mixture. Bake according to recipe directions.

To make crust for Topsy-Turvy Apple Pie (see page 17):

1. Remove one pie crust shell

from freezer. Invert crust onto waxed paper or insert. Let thaw until flattened, about 10 to 15 minutes. Keep second crust frozen until pie pan has been prepared.

2. Spread butter evenly on bottom and sides of the empty aluminum pie pan. Press pecan halves, rounded side down, into butter on bottom of pie pan. Pat brown sugar evenly over pecans.

3. Remove second pie crust from freezer. Lift crust from aluminum pan and place in first pie pan on top of brown sugar and pecans.

4. Fill and bake according to recipe instructions.

Topsy-Turvy Apple Pie (pictured above)

2 *Pet-Ritz* "Deep Dish" Pie
Crust Shells
¼ cup butter *or* margarine,
softened
½ cup *Funsten*® Pecan halves
½ cup packed brown sugar
5 large tart apples, pared, cored,
and sliced (about 6 cups)
1 tablespoon lemon juice
½ cup granulated sugar
1 tablespoon all-purpose flour
½ teaspoon ground cinnamon
½ teaspoon ground nutmeg

Prepare pie crust shell according to directions on opposite page. Set crust aside while preparing filling.

Sprinkle apple slices with lemon juice. Combine granulated sugar, flour, cinnamon, nutmeg, and a dash of *salt*; toss with apple slices. Spoon into pie shell; spread apples evenly to keep top level. Moisten edge of bottom crust with a little water.

Invert flattened crust over apple mixture, tuck edge under edge of lower crust to seal in juices. Flute edge. Prick top of pie with fork. Bake on preheated cookie sheet in 400° oven for 50 minutes. Remove from oven; cool 5 minutes. Place serving plate on top of pie; invert. Carefully remove pie pan. Serve warm.

Cut-and-Shape Crusts

When you have the urge to do something different with *Pet-Ritz* pastry, don't feel confined to the perameters of a pie pan. You can create a dozen different pastry treats, starting with a convenient frozen pie crust shell. You'll find recipes throughout this book for turnovers, tarts, flans, and other uniquely shaped pastries. You may even want to try some of your own favorites baked in a new crust.

Step by step

To make empty baked tart shells:

1. Remove pie crust shell from freezer. Invert frozen crust onto waxed paper or insert. Let thaw at room temperature until crust flattens, about 10 to 15 minutes.
2. Roll thawed crust lightly with rolling pin to a 14-inch circle, 1/16 inch thick. Cut into six 4½-inch circles.
3. Fit dough circles over inverted 2¾-inch muffin cups, pinching pleats at intervals to fit around cups. Prick pastry with a fork.
4. Bake in 450° oven for 7 to 10 minutes or until golden brown.

Let cool slightly; carefully lift off baked shell and invert onto wire rack to cool completely.
5. Fill shells according to recipe directions.

To make fill-and-bake tart shells:

1. Remove pie crust shell from freezer. Invert frozen crust onto waxed paper or insert. Let thaw at room temperature until crust flattens, about 10 to 15 minutes.
2. Roll thawed crust lightly with rolling pin to a 14-inch circle, about 1/16 inch thick. Cut into six 4½-inch circles.
3. Fit pastry circles into 2¾-inch muffin cups. Crimp edges.
4. Fill unbaked tart shells with prepared filling; bake according to recipe directions.
5. Remove from oven and cool on wire rack.

To make a 12-inch flan crust:

1. Remove pie crust shells from freezer. Invert frozen crusts onto waxed paper or insert. Let thaw at room temperature until flattened, about 10 to 15 minutes.
2. Invert one flattened crust directly on top of second flattened crust.
3. On waxed paper or lightly floured surface, roll both crusts firmly together with rolling pin to a 14-inch circle.
4. Transfer pastry circle to a 12-inch pizza pan. Turn edge under and crimp.
5. Prick crust and bake according to recipe directions.

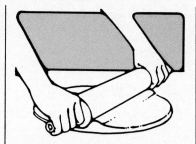

To make filled turnovers:

1. Remove pie crust from freezer. Invert frozen crust onto waxed paper or insert. Let thaw at room temperature until crust flattens, about 10 to 15 minutes.
2. Roll thawed crust lightly with rolling pin just until evenly flattened.
3. Spoon prepared filling into one half of pastry circle, spreading to within 1 inch of edge.
4. Fold opposite half of circle over filling; crimp edges with tines of fork to seal.
5. Prick with tines of fork, or cut several slits in top crust to allow steam to escape during baking.

Eggnog Tarts

2 *Pet-Ritz* "Deep Dish" Pie
   Crust Shells
2 tablespoons sugar
1 envelope unflavored gelatin
¼ teaspoon salt
⅛ teaspoon ground nutmeg
1 cup milk
3 slightly beaten egg yolks
¼ cup rum *or* brandy
3 egg whites
¼ cup sugar
½ cup whipping cream
   Candied cherries

Remove pie crusts from freezer. Invert onto waxed paper and let thaw 10 to 15 minutes. On a lightly floured surface roll each crust to a 14-inch circle, according to directions on page 18. Cut each circle into six 4½-inch rounds. Fit the pastry circles over inverted muffin cups. Prick pastry with a fork. Bake in 450° oven for 7 to 10 minutes or until golden brown. Cool. In saucepan combine the 2 tablespoons sugar, gelatin, salt, and nutmeg; stir in milk and yolks. Cook and stir until slightly thickened. Cool; stir in rum or brandy. Pour into large bowl; chill until partially set, stirring occasionally. Beat egg whites to soft peaks; gradually add ¼ cup sugar, beating to stiff peaks. Fold into gelatin mixture. Whip cream; fold in. Chill until mixture mounds. Spoon into tart shells; top each with a cherry. Chill. Makes 12.

Light lunches
quick as quiche

Whether it's Sunday morning brunch, midday lunch, or late-night snacking, we've got a quiche to suit the situation and satisfy everybody's taste. This basic cheese custard pie can range from the classic French version—Quiche Lorraine—to the contemporary adaptation pictured here—Italian Quiche. You'll find both recipes on pages 22–23—and they're followed by dozens more in this imaginative quiche chapter.

Italian Quiche (pictured on pages 20-21)

1 *Pet-Ritz* "Deep Dish" Pie
    Crust Shell
2 medium zucchini, chopped
    (2 cups)
1 medium onion, chopped
    (½ cup)
1 clove garlic, minced
2 tablespoons cooking oil
3 beaten eggs
1 cup cream-style cottage cheese
¾ cup milk
½ cup (2 ounces) shredded
    mozzarella cheese
1 can (16-ounce) tomatoes,
    undrained and cut up
1 can (8-ounce) tomato sauce
3 tablespoons snipped parsley

Prebake *unpricked* pie crust on preheated cookie sheet in 450° oven for 6 minutes (see page 6). Remove pie crust from oven. Reduce oven temperature to 325°.

Cook zucchini, onion, and garlic in hot oil just until tender, 8 to 10 minutes. Cool slightly. Spoon zucchini mixture into pastry shell. Combine eggs, cottage cheese, milk, and ½ teaspoon *salt*; spoon over zucchini. Bake in 325° oven on preheated cookie sheet for 45 minutes. Sprinkle with mozzarella; bake 5 minutes more or until knife inserted off center comes out clean. Let stand 10 minutes. Prepare *Herbed Tomato Sauce*: Combine tomatoes, tomato sauce, parsley, ½ teaspoon *salt*, a dash of *pepper*, and ½ teaspoon dried *oregano*, crushed. Bring to boiling; reduce heat. Cook, uncovered, until thickened, about 20 minutes. Cut quiche in wedges; top with sauce. Makes 6 servings.

Individual Chicken Quiches

1 *Pet-Ritz* "Deep Dish" Pie
    Crust Shell
2 eggs
¼ cup light cream
    Dash pepper
½ of a 4 ¾-ounce can chicken
    spread (about ¼ cup)
¾ cup (3 ounces) shredded
    gruyère cheese

Remove pie crust from freezer. Invert onto waxed paper or insert. Let thaw until flattened, about 10 to 15 minutes. Roll out the crust to a 14-inch circle, about 1/16 inch thick (see page 18). Cut pastry into twenty 2½-inch rounds. Fit into twenty 1¾-inch muffin cups.

Mix eggs, cream, and pepper. Fill each cup with ½ teaspoon chicken spread, a small amount cheese, and 1½ teaspoons egg mixture. Bake at 400° until golden, 18 to 20 minutes. Cool 1 minute; remove from pans. Makes 20.

Shallot Bacon Quiche

1 *Pet-Ritz* Regular Pie Crust
    Shell
6 slices bacon
¼ cup sliced shallots
1 cup (4 ounces) shredded
    natural Swiss cheese
3 beaten eggs
1 cup light cream
½ teaspoon salt
½ teaspoon dry mustard
    Dash ground nutmeg

Prebake *unpricked* pie crust on preheated cookie sheet in 450° oven for 6 minutes (see page 6). Remove from oven. Reduce temperature to 325°.

Crisp-cook bacon; crumble. Reserve 1 tablespoon drippings. Cook shallots in reserved drippings until tender. Set aside. Sprinkle cheese evenly over bottom of pastry shell; top with bacon and shallots. Combine remaining ingredients. Pour over cheese. Bake on preheated cookie sheet in 325° oven for 40 to 45 minutes or until knife inserted off center comes out clean. Let stand 10 minutes. Makes 6 servings.

Classic Quiche Lorraine (pictured above)

1 *Pet-Ritz* "Deep Dish" Pie
   Crust Shell
8 slices bacon
1 medium onion, thinly sliced
4 beaten eggs
1 cup light cream
1 cup milk
1 tablespoon all-purpose flour
½ teaspoon salt
   Dash ground nutmeg
1½ cups (6 ounces) shredded Swiss
   cheese

If desired, transfer frozen pie shell to quiche dish (see page 6). Prebake *unpricked* pie crust in 450° oven for 6 minutes. Remove pie crust from oven. Reduce temperature to 325°.

Crisp-cook bacon; crumble. Reserve 2 tablespoons drippings. Cook sliced onion in reserved drippings until tender; drain.

In bowl thoroughly stir together eggs, cream, milk, flour, salt, and nutmeg. Stir in finely crumbled bacon, onion, and cheese; mix well. Pour into pastry shell.

Bake on preheated cookie sheet in 325° oven for 45 to 50 minutes or until knife inserted off center comes out clean. Let stand 10 minutes before serving. Makes 6 servings.

Egg and Sausage Quiche (pictured on pages 4–5)

1 *Pet-Ritz* Regular Pie Crust
   Shell
8 ounces bulk pork sausage
3 hard-cooked eggs, chopped
½ cup (2 ounces) shredded
   natural Swiss cheese
½ cup (2 ounces) shredded
   natural cheddar cheese
2 beaten eggs
1 cup light cream *or* milk
¾ teaspoon salt
⅛ teaspoon pepper

Prebake *unpricked* pie crust on preheated cookie sheet in 450° oven for 6 minutes, according to directions on page 6. Remove pie crust from oven. Reduce oven temperature to 325°.

Cook sausage in skillet until brown, stirring with fork to break up meat. Drain well. Sprinkle hard-cooked egg in bottom of pastry shell; top with sausage and cheeses. Combine beaten eggs, cream, salt, and pepper; pour over all. Bake on preheated cookie sheet in 325° oven for 25 to 30 minutes or until knife inserted off center comes out clean. Let stand 10 minutes before serving. Garnish with additional egg slices, if desired. Makes 6 servings.

California Quiche

1 *Pet-Ritz* "Deep Dish" Pie
   Crust Shell
¾ pound hot Italian sausage
3 slightly beaten eggs
1¾ cups milk
2 cups (8 ounces) shredded
   monterey jack cheese
1 can (4-ounce) *Old El Paso*®
   Chopped Green Chilies
   (¼ cup)

Prebake *unpricked* pie crust on preheated cookie sheet in 450° oven for 6 minutes, according to directions on page 6. Remove pie crust from oven. Reduce oven temperature to 325°.

Crumble sausage, removing from casing if necessary. Cook sausage in skillet until brown, breaking up meat with a fork. Drain well. In mixing bowl combine eggs, milk, sausage, cheese and chilies. Turn into partially baked pastry shell. Bake in 325° oven on preheated cookie sheet 45 minutes or until knife inserted off center comes out clean. Let stand about 10 minutes before serving. Makes 6 servings.

Turkey Quiche

1 *Pet-Ritz* "Deep Dish" Pie
   Crust Shell
1 cup finely chopped cooked
   turkey
1 can (3-ounce) sliced mushrooms, drained
¾ cup (3 ounces) shredded
   American cheese
1 can (10½-ounce) condensed
   cream of shrimp soup
¼ cup milk
4 eggs

Prebake *unpricked* pie crust on preheated cookie sheet in 450° oven for 6 minutes, according to directions on page 6. Remove pie crust from oven. Reduce oven temperature to 325°.

Arrange turkey and mushrooms in bottom of pastry shell. Sprinkle cheese over top. In small saucepan combine soup and milk; heat mixture just to boiling, stirring constantly. In large mixing bowl beat eggs until blended. Gradually stir hot mixture into beaten eggs. Pour soup mixture over cheese in pastry shell. Bake on preheated cookie sheet in 325° oven 40 to 45 minutes or until knife inserted off center comes out clean. Let stand 10 minutes. Makes 6 servings.

Pizza Quiche

2 *Pet-Ritz* "Deep Dish" Pie
  Crust Shells
1 cup (8 ounces) ricotta *or*
  cream-style cottage cheese
3 eggs
4 ounces Italian sausage, cooked
  and drained
1 cup (4 ounces) shredded
  mozzarella cheese
½ cup sliced pepperoni, halved
½ cup diced prosciutto *or* fully
  cooked ham
½ cup sliced salami cut in strips
¼ cup grated parmesan cheese
1 beaten egg
2 tablespoons milk

Remove pie crusts from freezer. Invert one crust onto waxed paper and let thaw 10 to 15 minutes (see page 8). Prebake *unpricked* pie crust on preheated cookie sheet in 450° oven for 6 minutes, according to directions on page 6. Remove pie crust from oven. Reduce oven temperature to 350°.

Beat together ricotta cheese and 3 eggs; fold in sausage, mozzarella, pepperoni, prosciutto, salami, and parmesan cheese. Turn into pastry shell.

Cut flattened pie crust in 6 wedges. Arrange wedges on top of filling. Bake pie on preheated cookie sheet in 350° oven for 20 minutes.

Combine the 1 egg and milk; brush over pastry wedges. Bake until golden, about 20 minutes. Let stand about 10 minutes. Makes 6 servings.

Confetti Cheese Quiche

1 *Pet-Ritz* Regular Pie Crust
  Shell
1 can (8-ounce) mixed vegetables, drained
¼ cup finely chopped green onion
1 cup (4 ounces) shredded
  American cheese
3 slightly beaten eggs
1 cup milk
½ teaspoon salt
⅛ teaspoon pepper

Prebake *unpricked* pie crust on preheated cookie sheet in 450° oven for 6 minutes (see page 6). Remove from oven. Reduce temperature to 325°.

In small bowl combine drained vegetables and onion. Sprinkle *half* of the cheese over the bottom of the pastry shell. Top with the vegetable mixture. In large bowl combine beaten eggs, milk, salt, and pepper. Pour egg mixture over vegetables. Sprinkle with remaining cheese. Bake on preheated cookie sheet in 325° oven for 45 minutes or until knife inserted off center comes out clean. Remove pie from oven and let stand 10 minutes before serving. Makes 6 servings.

ABC Quiche

1 *Pet-Ritz* "Deep Dish" Pie
  Crust Shell
8 ounces fresh asparagus, cut up
4 ounces Canadian bacon, cut in
  ½-inch cubes
1 cup (4 ounces) shredded
  gruyère cheese
3 beaten eggs
1 cup milk
½ teaspoon salt
⅛ teaspoon ground nutmeg

Prebake *unpricked* pie crust on preheated cookie sheet in 450° oven for 6 minutes (see page 6). Remove pie crust from oven. Reduce oven to 325°.

Cook asparagus in boiling salted water 8 to 10 minutes. Drain. Place asparagus and Canadian bacon in pastry shell. Sprinkle cheese on top.

In mixing bowl combine the eggs, milk, salt, and nutmeg; pour into pastry shell. Bake on preheated cookie sheet in 325° oven for 45 minutes or until knife inserted off center comes out clean. Let stand 10 minutes. Makes 6 servings.

Chili Cheese Quiche (pictured right)

1 *Pet-Ritz* "Deep Dish" Pie
    Crust Shell
1½ cups (6 ounces) shredded
    monterey jack cheese
8 ounces Italian sausage *or*
    chorizo, cooked and drained
2 tablespoons *Old El Paso*
    Chopped Green Chilies
3 eggs
1 cup light cream
½ teaspoon salt
    Tomato and avocado wedges
    Parsley sprigs

If desired, transfer frozen pie shell to glass or ceramic pie plate or quiche dish (see page 6). Prebake *unpricked* pie crust on preheated cookie sheet in 450° oven for 6 minutes. Remove pie crust from oven. Reduce oven temperature to 325°.

Sprinkle *1 cup* of cheese in bottom of pie shell. Top with sausage and chilies. Put eggs, cream, and salt in food processor or blender container; process until smooth. Pour over sausage. Bake on preheated cookie sheet in 325° oven for 30 to 35 minutes or until knife inserted off center comes out clean. Top with tomato and avocado wedges, if desired. Sprinkle with remaining cheese. Bake 2 minutes longer. Let stand 10 minutes. Makes 6 servings.

Easy Rarebit Wedges

1 *Pet-Ritz* Regular Pie Crust
    Shell
3 slightly beaten eggs
1 package (10-ounce) frozen
    Welsh rarebit, partially
    thawed
⅛ teaspoon pepper
5 slices bacon, crisp-cooked and
    drained

Prebake *unpricked* pie crust on preheated cookie sheet in 450° oven for 6 minutes (see page 6). Remove from oven. Reduce temperature to 350°.

Put eggs in food processor or blender container; process until foamy. Break rarebit in pieces into container with eggs; add pepper. Process until combined. Add bacon; process until coarsely chopped. Pour mixture into pie shell. Bake on preheated cookie sheet in 350° oven until knife inserted off center comes out clean, about 40 minutes. Let stand 10 minutes. Makes 6 servings.

Pepperoni Tarts

1 *Pet-Ritz* "Deep Dish" Pie
    Crust Shell
½ cup milk
2 eggs
2 ounces sliced pepperoni
1 slice (1 ounce) American
    cheese, cut in pieces
    (¼ cup)
¼ small onion, cut in pieces
¼ teaspoon salt

Remove pie crust from freezer. Invert onto waxed paper or lightly floured surface and let thaw 10 to 15 minutes. Roll pastry to a 14-inch circle (see page 18). Cut into six 4½-inch circles. Fit pastry into greased muffin cups; crimp edges. Prick pastry with fork. Bake in 400° oven until golden brown, about 10 minutes. Remove tarts from oven; reduce oven temperature to 325°.

Put milk, eggs, pepperoni, cheese, onion pieces, and the salt in food processor or blender container. Process until pepperoni is finely chopped. Spoon filling into tarts. Bake in 325° oven until knife inserted off center comes out clean, 12 minutes. Cool slightly; carefully remove from pan. Serve warm. Makes 6 servings.

Quick Tips

Blender/Food Processor Tips

If you have a blender or food processor, you can save yourself a lot of time and energy by preparing your quiche fillings all in one container. Just combine the eggs, milk or cream, and seasonings in the blender or processor container, and process until well blended. If other ingredients are to be added, such as cheese, meat, vegetables, or nuts, they can be added in coarse chunks with the custard mixture and chopped during processing.

If you prefer to chop, slice, or shred additional ingredients sep-

arately, do them first while the container is dry. Turn the motor off and on quickly when chopping to regulate the size of particles. To help achieve a uniform chop, do not put more than 2 cups of food in the container at once, and cut the food in fairly uniform size pieces to start. For the blender, fruits, vegetables, and cooked meats should be in ½- to 1-inch pieces, and cheese should be in ½-inch cubes; for a food processor, the pieces can be somewhat larger. Turn the machine off before using a rubber spatula or other small utensil to scrape food

down from the sides of the container into the range of the blade.

To save time and dishwashing, consolidate several preparations in one procedure, or process frequently used foods in quantity and store them in the freezer or refrigerator. You can also process foods of similar texture in one step, such as onion and green pepper.

With a little practice, you'll quickly learn to think in terms of food processors and blenders, and thereby mentally reorganize your recipes to save yourself the most time and effort.

Swiss Ham Pie

1 *Pet-Ritz* Regular Pie Crust
  Shell
2 tablespoons butter *or*
  margarine
2 tablespoons all-purpose flour
⅛ teaspoon ground nutmeg
1½ cups milk
1 cup (4 ounces) shredded
  Swiss cheese
3 slightly beaten eggs
1 cup diced cooked ham

Prebake *unpricked* pie crust on preheated cookie sheet in 450° oven for 6 minutes, according to directions on page 6. Remove pie crust from oven. Reduce oven temperature to 325°.

In medium saucepan melt butter or margarine; blend in flour and nutmeg. Add milk all at once; cook and stir until thick and bubbly. Add cheese; stir until melted. Cool slightly; stir small amount of cheese sauce into eggs. Return egg mixture to cheese sauce; add ham. Pour into partially baked shell.

Bake on preheated cookie sheet in 325° oven for 45 to 50 minutes. Let stand 10 minutes before serving. Makes 6 servings.

Ham and Egg Quiche

1 *Pet-Ritz* "Deep Dish" Pie
  Crust Shell
4 hard-cooked eggs, chopped
½ pound ground ham
1 cup (4 ounces) shredded Swiss
  cheese
1 cup (4 ounces) shredded
  cheddar cheese
3 eggs, beaten
1¼ cups light cream
⅛ teaspoon pepper

Prebake *unpricked* pie crust on preheated cookie sheet in 450° oven for 6 minutes, according to directions on page 6. Remove pie crust from oven. Reduce oven temperature to 350°. Sprinkle hard-cooked eggs in bottom of partially baked pastry shell. Top with ham and cheeses. Combine beaten eggs, cream, and pepper. Pour over filling. Bake on preheated cookie sheet in 350° oven for 30 to 35 minutes or until knife inserted off center comes out clean. Let stand 10 minutes before serving. Makes 6 servings.

Leek Quiche

1 *Pet-Ritz* "Deep Dish" Pie
  Crust Shell
8 slices bacon
1 cup sliced leeks (2 large leeks)
2 cups (8 ounces) shredded natural Swiss cheese
3 beaten eggs
1½ cups milk
1 tablespoon all-purpose flour
½ teaspoon salt
  Dash ground nutmeg

Prebake *unpricked* pie crust on a preheated cookie sheet in 450° oven for 6 minutes, according to directions on page 6. Remove pie crust from oven. Reduce oven temperature to 325°.

In skillet crisp cook bacon. Drain, reserving 2 tablespoons drippings in skillet. Crumble bacon and set aside. Cook leeks in reserved drippings until tender; drain. Place all but 2 tablespoons of the bacon in partially baked shell; top with cheese and leeks. Combine eggs and milk; with rotary beater, beat in flour, salt, and nutmeg. Pour mixture into pastry shell. Sprinkle with reserved bacon. Bake on preheated cookie sheet in 325° oven for 45 minutes or until knife inserted off center comes out clean. Let cool 10 minutes before serving. Makes 6 servings.

Swiss 'n Frank Pie

1 *Pet-Ritz* "Deep Dish" Pie
   Crust Shell
¼ cup finely chopped onion
1 tablespoon butter *or* margarine
2 cups thinly sliced franks
   (5 to 6 franks)
1 cup (4 ounces) shredded process Swiss cheese
3 slightly beaten eggs
1½ cups milk
1 teaspoon dry mustard
½ teaspoon salt
¼ teaspoon ground nutmeg

Prebake *unpricked* pie crust on preheated cookie sheet in 450° oven for 6 minutes, according to directions on page 6. Remove from oven. Reduce oven temperature to 325°.

Cook onion in butter or margarine until tender. Place franks, cheese, and cooked onion in partially baked pastry shell. Combine eggs, milk, dry mustard, salt, nutmeg, and a dash of *pepper*; pour over frank mixture. Bake on preheated cookie sheet in 325° oven for 35 to 40 minutes or until knife inserted off center comes out clean. Let cool 10 minutes before serving. Makes 6 servings.

Hamburger Mini Quiche

1 *Pet-Ritz* "Deep Dish" Pie
   Crust Shell
½ pound ground beef
½ cup (2 ounces) shredded Swiss
   cheese
2 tablespoons finely chopped
   onion
2 slightly beaten eggs
½ cup dairy sour cream
½ teaspoon Worcestershire sauce
¼ teaspoon salt

Remove pie crust shell from freezer. Invert onto waxed paper or insert. Let thaw until flattened, about 10 to 15 minutes. Roll out the crust to a 14-inch circle, about ¹⁄₁₆ inch thick, according to directions on page 18. Cut into twenty 2½-inch circles. Fit into 1¾-inch muffin pans.

In skillet brown beef over medium heat, stirring with fork to break up meat. Drain. Mix beef, cheese, and onion. Fill cups half full with meat-cheese mixture. Combine eggs, sour cream, Worcestershire sauce, and salt. Spoon 2 teaspoons mixture into each cup. Bake in 375° oven for 30 minutes; cool in pans 5 minutes before removing. Serve warm. Makes 20.

Sausage and Mushroom Quiche

1 *Pet-Ritz* "Deep Dish" Pie
   Crust Shell
3 slightly beaten eggs
1 tall can (13 fl. oz.) *Pet*
   Evaporated Milk
4 ounces (about ¾ cup) smoked
   sausage, chopped
1 can (2-ounce) sliced mushrooms, drained
1 cup (4 ounces) shredded
   muenster cheese
1 tablespoon all-purpose flour
¼ teaspoon salt

Prebake *unpricked* pie crust on preheated cookie sheet in 450° oven for 6 minutes, according to directions on page 6. Remove pie crust from oven. Reduce oven temperature to 325°.

In bowl combine eggs, evaporated milk, sausage, and mushrooms. Toss flour with cheese; add to egg mixture along with salt. Pour mixture into partially baked pastry shell. Bake on preheated cookie sheet until knife inserted off center comes out clean, 30 to 35 minutes. Let stand 10 minutes before serving. Makes 6 servings.

Spinach Quiche

1 *Pet-Ritz* "Deep Dish" Pie
   Crust Shell
3 tablespoons chopped onion
2 tablespoons butter
1 tablespoon all-purpose flour
1 package (10-ounce) frozen
   chopped spinach, cooked
   and drained
1 cup shredded Swiss cheese
¼ cup grated parmesan cheese
3 slightly beaten eggs
1½ cups light cream
1 teaspoon salt

Prebake *unpricked* pie crust on preheated cookie sheet in 450° oven for 6 minutes, according to directions on page 6. Remove pie crust from oven. Reduce oven temperature to 325°.

In saucepan cook onion in butter until tender but not brown. Blend in flour. Stir in spinach and cheeses. Spread in partially baked pastry shell. Mix together eggs, cream, and salt. Pour over spinach mixture. Bake on preheated cookie sheet in 325° oven until knife inserted off center comes out clean, 40 to 45 minutes. Let stand 10 minutes before serving. Makes 6 servings.

Quick Frank Quiche

1 *Pet-Ritz* Regular Pie Crust Shell
1 can (3-ounce) French-fried onions
6 ounces frankfurters, sliced
1 cup (4 ounces) shredded
   mozzarella cheese
2 beaten eggs
1 small can (5.33 fl. oz.) *Pet*
   Evaporated Milk
½ teaspoon dry mustard
½ teaspoon dried parsley flakes
¼ teaspoon salt

Prebake *unpricked* pie crust on preheated cookie sheet in 450° oven for 6 minutes, according to directions on page 6. Remove pie crust from oven. Reduce oven temperature to 325°. Sprinkle *half* the onion over bottom of partially baked pastry shell; top with sliced frankfurters and cheese. Mix eggs, evaporated milk, mustard, parsley, and salt. Pour over cheese. Bake on preheated cookie sheet in 325° oven 45 minutes. Top with remaining onion during last 5 minutes. Makes 6 servings.

Mushroom Onion Quiche

1 *Pet-Ritz* "Deep Dish" Pie
   Crust Shell
1½ cups sliced fresh mushrooms
¾ cup chopped onion
2 tablespoons butter *or*
   margarine
¼ teaspoon salt
1½ cups (6 ounces) shredded
   natural Swiss cheese
4 beaten eggs
¾ cup whipping cream
¾ cup milk
½ teaspoon salt
   Dash pepper

Prebake *unpricked* pie crust on preheated cookie sheet in 450° oven for 6 minutes, according to directions on page 6. Remove pie crust from oven. Reduce oven temperature to 325°. Cook mushrooms and onion in butter or margarine until onion is tender, but not brown. Drain; sprinkle with ¼ teaspoon salt. Sprinkle cheese over bottom of partially baked pastry shell. Spoon mushroom mixture over cheese.

Combine eggs, cream, milk, ½ teaspoon salt, and dash pepper. Pour into pastry shell. Bake on preheated cookie sheet in 325° oven for 50 minutes or until knife inserted off center comes out clean. Let stand 10 minutes before serving. Makes 6 servings.

French Onion Pie (pictured above)

1 *Pet-Ritz* "Deep Dish" Pie
  Crust Shell
1 can (3-ounce) French-fried
  onions
4 eggs
2 cups milk
½ cup (2 ounces) shredded sharp
  American cheese
½ teaspoon salt
  Dash cayenne
1 cup (4 ounces) shredded sharp
  American cheese

If desired, transfer frozen pie shell to glass or ceramic pie plate, according to directions on page 6.

Prebake *unpricked* pie crust in 450° oven for 6 minutes. Remove pie crust from oven. Reduce oven temperature to 325°.

Fill bottom of partially baked pie shell with 1½ cups of the French-fried onions. Beat eggs slightly; blend in milk, the ½ cup shredded American cheese, the salt, and cayenne. Pour over French-fried onions. Sprinkle the 1 cup shredded American cheese over pie. Bake on preheated cookie sheet in 325° oven for 45 minutes. Sprinkle remaining onions around edge of pie. Bake until knife inserted just off center comes out clean, about 5 to 10 minutes more. Let stand at room temperature 10 minutes before serving. Makes 6 servings.

Seafood Quiche

1 *Pet-Ritz* Regular Pie Crust
    Shell
½ cup chopped onion
2 tablespoons butter *or* margarine
3 beaten eggs
¾ cup light cream
¾ cup milk
½ teaspoon shredded lemon peel
    Dash nutmeg
1 can (7½-ounce) crab meat,
    drained and flaked *or* 1 can
    (4½-ounce) shrimp, drained
    and chopped
1½ cups shredded Swiss cheese
1 tablespoon all-purpose flour
¼ cup sliced *Funsten* Almonds

Prebake *unpricked* pie crust on preheated cookie sheet in 450° oven for 6 minutes, according to directions on page 6. Remove pie crust from oven. Reduce oven temperature to 325°.

In small saucepan cook onion in the butter or margarine until tender. In bowl stir together the eggs, cream, milk, cooked onion, ½ teaspoon *salt*, lemon peel, and nutmeg. Add shrimp or crab. Combine shredded cheese and the flour; add to mixture. Pour into pastry shell. Top with sliced almonds. Bake on preheated cookie sheet in 325° oven until knife inserted off center comes out clean, about 35 to 40 minutes. Let stand 10 minutes. Makes 6 servings.

Crab Quiche Florentine

1 *Pet-Ritz* "Deep Dish" Pie
    Crust Shell
1 package (10-ounce) frozen
    chopped spinach
3 slightly beaten eggs
1¼ cups milk
1 can (7½-ounce) crab meat,
    drained, flaked, and cartilage
    removed
1½ cups shredded Swiss cheese
2 tablespoons grated parmesan
    cheese
    Several dashes paprika

Prebake *unpricked* pie crust on preheated cookie sheet in 450° oven for 6 minutes (see page 6). Remove from oven. Reduce temperature to 325°.

Cook spinach according to package directions. Drain well, pressing out excess water. Combine eggs, milk, drained spinach, crab meat, and cheese. Pour into partially baked pastry shell. Top with parmesan cheese; sprinkle with paprika.

Bake on preheated cookie sheet in 325° oven for 45 to 50 minutes or until knife inserted off center comes out clean. Let stand 10 minutes before serving. Makes 6 servings.

Shrimp Tarts

2 *Pet-Ritz* "Deep Dish" Pie
    Crust Shells
3 eggs
1½ cups (12 ounces) cream-style
    cottage cheese
1 can (8½-ounce) peas, drained
    Dash pepper
1 can (4½-ounce) shrimp,
    drained and rinsed

Remove pie crusts from freezer. Invert onto waxed paper or lightly floured surface, and let thaw 10 to 15 minutes. Roll each crust to a 14-inch circle ¹⁄₁₆ inch thick (see page 18). Cut each into six 4½-inch circles. Fit pastry into 2¾-inch muffin cups; crimp edges.

Beat eggs until foamy; stir in cottage cheese, peas, and pepper. Stir shrimp into egg mixture. Turn into prepared pastry shells. Bake in 350° oven 20 to 25 minutes. Let stand 5 minutes. Makes 12 tarts.

Scrambled Egg Pie

1 *Pet-Ritz* Regular Pie Crust
  Shell
2 slices bacon
10 eggs
⅓ cup milk
1 tablespoon Dijon-style mustard
½ teaspoon salt
  Dash pepper
2 tablespoons chopped green
  onion
4 tablespoons butter *or*
  margarine
½ cup (2 ounces) shredded sharp
  American cheese

Thaw pie crust 10 minutes. Prick bottom and sides thoroughly with tines of fork. Bake on preheated cookie sheet in 400° oven for 10 minutes (see page 6). Remove pie crust from oven; cool.

In 10-inch skillet crisp-cook bacon. Drain and crumble bacon; set aside. In bowl beat eggs, milk, mustard, salt, and pepper. In same skillet cook onion in butter or margarine until tender but not brown. Add egg mixture. Cook slowly, lifting and turning cooked egg portion with spatula to allow uncooked portion to flow underneath. When eggs are almost set, spoon into pastry shell. Sprinkle bacon, then cheese on top. Bake in 350° oven for 5 minutes more or until cheese melts. Garnish top of pie with bacon curls and parsley, if desired. Makes 6 servings.

Cheesy Brunch Quiche

1 *Pet-Ritz* "Deep Dish" Pie
  Crust Shell
2 slightly beaten eggs
1 cup dairy sour cream
8 ounces bacon, cooked, drained
  and crumbled
1 cup (4 ounces) shredded Swiss
  cheese
2 tablespoons snipped parsley

Place frozen pie crust in a 9-inch round quiche dish. Let crust thaw 10 to 15 minutes. Gently press pastry to mold to dish. Bake *unpricked* crust in 450° oven for 6 minutes according to directions on page 6. Remove pie crust from oven. Reduce temperature to 425°.

Meanwhile stir together eggs, sour cream, bacon, cheese, and parsley. Pour into pie crust shell. Bake in 425° oven until cheese puffs and is lightly browned, about 18 to 20 minutes. Makes 6 servings.

Salmon Quiche

1 *Pet-Ritz* "Deep Dish" Pie
  Crust Shell
1 can (15½-ounce) salmon
3 beaten eggs
1 cup dairy sour cream
¼ cup mayonnaise *or* salad
  dressing
½ cup (2 ounces) shredded sharp
  cheddar cheese
1 tablespoon grated onion
¼ teaspoon dried dillweed
3 drops bottled hot pepper sauce

Prebake *unpricked* pie crust on preheated cookie sheet in 450° oven for 6 minutes, according to directions on page 6. Remove pie crust from oven. Reduce oven temperature to 325°.

Meanwhile, for filling, drain salmon, reserving liquid. Add water to reserved liquid, if necessary, to make ½ cup liquid. Flake salmon, removing bones and skin; set aside. In a bowl blend together beaten eggs, sour cream, mayonnaise or salad dressing, and reserved salmon liquid. Stir in salmon, shredded cheese, the grated onion, dillweed, and hot pepper sauce. Spoon filling into crust. Bake on preheated cookie sheet in 325° oven 45 minutes or until set. Makes 6 servings.

Enticing entrées under a crust

Looking for a tantalizing lunch or supper dish? Explore these surprising entrées baked in a blanket of *Pet-Ritz* pastry. There's no end to the delicious meat, fish, or poultry fillings that can tuck inside a main dish pie, hide beneath a casserole crust, or fold into a flaky turnover.

Burgers Wellington are an elegant, but economical, knock-off of the classic English entrée. You'll find the traditional flavors—beef, pâté, mushrooms, and herbs—inside this golden crust covering. Turn the page for this and more exciting main dish ideas.

Roast Beef a la Wellington (pictured right)

1 3- to 3½-pound beef eye of
   round roast
¾ cup burgundy
¾ cup dry sherry
1 medium onion, sliced
2 bay leaves
1½ cups chopped fresh mushrooms
1 leek, chopped (¼ cup)
1 tablespoon butter *or* margarine
¼ cup liver pâté *or* ½ of a
   4¾-ounce can liver spread
2 tablespoons fine dry bread
   crumbs
2 *Pet-Ritz* "Deep Dish" Pie
   Crust Shells
1 beaten egg
¾ cup water
½ cup cold water
3 tablespoons all-purpose flour
   Salt
   Pepper

Place meat in plastic bag; set in deep bowl. Combine burgundy, sherry, onion, and bay leaves. Pour over meat; close. Chill overnight; turn bag occasionally. Next day, remove meat. Strain marinade; reserve ¼ cup. Place meat on rack in shallow roasting pan. Insert meat thermometer. Roast, uncovered, in 425° oven until thermometer registers 130°, about 55 minutes. Remove meat from pan; cool 20 minutes. Reserve drippings in pan. Trim fat from meat. Cook mushrooms and leek in butter until tender and liquid has evaporated. Remove from heat; stir in pâté and crumbs. Cover and chill.

Remove crusts from freezer. Invert crusts onto a floured surface; let thaw until flattened, 10 to 15 minutes. Place one crust on top of the other. Roll together to make a rectangle 12×16 inches. From one end cut eight 12-inch strips ½ inch wide; set aside. Place meat on greased baking sheet. Spread with pâté mixture. Place 12-inch pastry square over meat; tuck ends and sides under. Brush egg over all. Crisscross pastry strips over roast. Brush with remaining egg. Bake in 450° oven 15 minutes (meat will be rare). Add ¾ cup water to pan drippings; heat and stir until solids dissolve. Blend cold water and flour; stir into drippings with reserved marinade. Cook and stir until bubbly. Season with salt and pepper. Serve with roast. Makes 12 servings.

Burgers Wellington (pictured on pages 34–35)

2 beaten eggs
½ cup milk
1½ cups soft bread crumbs (2 slices
   bread)
2 tablespoons finely chopped
   onion
1 teaspoon Worcestershire sauce
½ teaspoon dried thyme, crushed
   Dash pepper
2 pounds lean ground beef
3 *Pet-Ritz* Regular Pie Crust Shells
1 can (4¾-ounce) liver spread
1 can (3-ounce) sliced mushrooms, drained
1 slightly beaten egg
1 tablespoon water

Combine 2 beaten eggs, milk, bread crumbs, onion, 1 teaspoon *salt*, Worcestershire, thyme, and pepper. Add ground beef; mix well. Shape into 8 patties, 3 inches in diameter. Place in baking pan. Bake in 350° oven for 30 minutes. Remove pie crust shells from freezer. Invert crusts onto waxed paper and let thaw until flattened, about 10 to 15 minutes.

Remove patties from oven; let cool 5 minutes. Increase oven temperature to 450°. Transfer patties to clean baking pan. Top each with ½ tablespoon of liver spread and a few mushrooms. Cut each crust into 3 equal wedges. Place one wedge of pastry over each patty; tuck ends under. Brush with mixture of beaten egg and water. Decorate with small cutouts made from remaining pastry wedge. Bake at 450° for 12 to 15 minutes or until golden. Makes 8 servings.

Jiffy Wellington Pie

1 slightly beaten egg
¼ cup water
2 tablespoons dry red wine
2 cups soft bread crumbs
   (2½ slices bread)
1 teaspoon salt
⅛ teaspoon pepper
¼ teaspoon dried thyme, crushed
1½ pounds ground beef
1 *Pet-Ritz* "Deep Dish" Pie
   Crust Shell
1 can (4¾-ounce) liver spread
1 can (3-ounce) sliced
   mushrooms, drained
1 envelope (1⅛-ounce)
   Hollandaise sauce mix

Combine egg, water, wine, bread crumbs, salt, pepper, and thyme. Add ground beef; mix well. Press into a 9-inch pie plate. Bake in 350° oven for 40 minutes.

Meanwhile, remove pie crust from freezer. Invert onto waxed paper and let thaw 10 to 15 minutes, according to directions on page 8. Drain excess juices from meat; invert onto oven-proof platter. Set oven at 450°. Spread meat with liver spread; top with the mushroom slices. Place flattened pie crust carefully over meat. Press edges of crust to platter to seal in meat. Cut slits in top for escape of steam. Bake in 450° oven for 15 minutes or until golden. Prepare Hollandaise sauce mix according to package directions. Transfer meat to serving plate. Spoon Hollandaise sauce over each serving. Makes 6 servings.

Beef Pie with Caper Sauce

2 *Pet-Ritz* "Deep Dish" Pie
　　Crust Shells
¼ cup chopped onion
1 tablespoon butter *or* margarine
3 tablespoons all-purpose flour
1 teaspoon instant beef bouillon
　　granules
¼ teaspoon ground nutmeg
⅛ teaspoon pepper
1 cup water
1 tablespoon anchovy paste
1 tablespoon chopped capers
2 cups finely chopped cooked
　　beef
1 recipe Caper Sauce

Remove pie crusts from freezer. Invert one crust onto waxed paper and let thaw 10 to 15 minutes, according to directions on page 8.

Cook onion in butter or margarine until tender but not brown. Blend flour, bouillon granules, nutmeg, and pepper into onion mixture. Stir in water. Cook over medium heat, stirring constantly, until thickened and bubbly. Stir in anchovy paste and capers. Add beef; mix well.

Spoon the hot meat mixture into the second crust in pie pan. Moisten edge of pie crust with a little water. Invert flattened crust on top of filling; tuck edge under and crimp. Cut slits in top crust for escape of steam. Bake on preheated cookie sheet in 350° oven for 50 to 60 minutes. Let stand about 10 minutes. Serve with Caper Sauce. Serves 6.

Caper Sauce: In saucepan melt 2 tablespoons *butter or margarine*. Blend in 2 tablespoons all-purpose *flour*, 1 teaspoon instant chicken *bouillon granules*, and ½ teaspoon *Worcestershire sauce*. Stir in 1 cup *water*. Cook and stir until bubbly. Stir in 1 tablespoon *capers*. Makes 1 cup.

Beef and Kidney Pie

1 pound beef *or* veal kidney
1 medium onion, sliced
⅓ cup dry red wine
4 bay leaves
3 whole black peppercorns
½ teaspoon salt
2 pounds beef round steak, cut in
　　1-inch cubes
½ cup all-purpose flour
½ cup chopped onion
3 tablespoons shortening, melted
¼ cup snipped parsley
¼ cup chopped celery leaves
1 teaspoon dried marjoram,
　　crushed
1½ cups water
1 cup sliced fresh mushrooms
1 *Pet-Ritz* Regular Pie Crust
　　Shell
2 tablespoons all-purpose flour
　　Milk

Remove any membrane and hard white parts from kidney; cut in 1-inch pieces. Mix kidney, sliced onion, wine, three bay leaves, peppercorns, and salt; marinate mixture at room temperature for 1 hour. Coat steak cubes with part of the ½ cup flour. In Dutch oven brown steak cubes and chopped onion in shortening. Drain kidney, reserving ⅓ cup marinade. Strain marinade; set aside. Coat kidney with remainder of ½ cup flour. Add to beef. Cook, uncovered, 5 minutes. Stir in parsley, celery leaves, marjoram, remaining bay leaf, and 1½ cups water. Cover; simmer until meat is tender, about 1½ hours.

Remove pie crust from freezer. Invert onto waxed paper and let thaw until flattened, 10 to 15 minutes. Stir mushrooms into meat mixture; cook 5 minutes. Blend reserved marinade into 2 tablespoons flour. Stir into meat mixture. Cook and stir until bubbly. Remove bay leaf. Pour into 2-quart casserole. Invert crust on top of filling; crimp edge to lip of dish. Cut slits for escape of steam; brush with milk. Bake in 450° oven about 20 minutes. Makes 6 servings.

Beef Steak Pie

1½ pounds beef round steak, cut in
    1-inch cubes
¼ cup all-purpose flour
1 large onion, cut in pieces
2 tablespoons shortening
2 cups water
1 teaspoon salt
¼ teaspoon dried thyme, crushed
⅛ teaspoon pepper
2 cups diced raw potato
1 *Pet-Ritz* Regular Pie Crust Shell
    Milk

Toss beef with flour to coat. In saucepan cook beef and onion in shortening until beef is browned and onion is tender. Add water, salt, thyme, and pepper. Cover; simmer 1½ hours. Add potato. Cover; simmer 20 minutes.

Remove pie crust from freezer. Invert onto waxed paper and let thaw until flattened, 10 to 15 minutes.

Turn meat into a 1½-quart casserole. Invert flattened crust on top of filling. Crimp edge to lip of dish. Brush top crust with milk. Bake in 450° oven until golden, about 15 minutes. Makes 6 servings.

Pork and Apple Pie (pictured on pages 4–5)

2 *Pet-Ritz* "Deep Dish" Pie
    Crust Shells
1 pound lean ground pork
1 medium onion, finely chopped
    (½ cup)
½ cup fine dry bread crumbs
½ cup chicken broth
1 teaspoon salt
    Dash pepper
2 medium cooking apples, peeled,
    cored, and sliced (2 cups)
2 tablespoons brown sugar
¼ teaspoon ground cinnamon

Remove pie crusts from freezer. Invert one crust onto waxed paper and let thaw 10 to 15 minutes, according to directions on page 8.

In skillet cook pork and onion until pork is browned and onion is tender. Remove from heat. Stir in bread crumbs, chicken broth, salt, and pepper. Pour filling into second crust in pie pan. Combine apples, brown sugar, and cinnamon; spoon on top of meat layer. Moisten edge of crust with a little water. Invert flattened crust on top of filling; tuck edge under and crimp. Cut slits in top crust for steam to escape. Bake on preheated cookie sheet in 400° oven for 35 to 40 minutes or until golden brown. Let stand 10 minutes before serving. Makes 6 servings.

Canadian Pork Pie

1 pound ground pork
1 cup water
½ cup finely chopped onion
½ cup fine dry bread crumbs
¾ teaspoon salt
    Dash pepper
    Dash ground sage
    Dash ground nutmeg
2 *Pet-Ritz* "Deep Dish" Pie
    Crust Shells

Brown the pork in skillet; drain off excess fat. Add water, onion, crumbs, and seasonings. Simmer, covered, 30 minutes, stirring occasionally. Meanwhile, remove pie crusts from freezer. Invert one crust onto waxed paper and let thaw 10 to 15 minutes, according to directions on page 8. Turn meat mixture into second crust in pie pan. Moisten edge of crust with a little water. Invert flattened crust on top of filling; tuck edge under and crimp. Cut slits in top for escape of steam. Bake on preheated cookie sheet in 400° oven until crust is golden brown, about 35 minutes. Makes 6 servings.

Enticing entrées/Meat pies and pastries

Cheesy Beef Pie (pictured right)

2 *Pet-Ritz* "Deep Dish" Pie
  Crust Shells
1 pound ground beef
½ cup chopped onion
2 teaspoons cornstarch
1 can (10-ounce) *Old El Paso*
  Mild Enchilada Sauce
¼ cup snipped parsley
1 can (3-ounce) chopped mushrooms, drained
2 eggs
1 egg white
6 slices (6 ounces) sharp
  American cheese
1 egg yolk
1 tablespoon water

Remove pie crusts from freezer. Invert one crust onto waxed paper and let thaw until flattened, 10 to 15 minutes. If desired, transfer second pie crust to glass or ceramic pie plate, according to directions on page 6.

In skillet brown beef and onion; drain. Sprinkle with cornstarch; blend in. Stir in enchilada sauce, parsley, and mushrooms; set aside. Beat together two eggs and egg white; spread half over crust in pie plate. Spoon meat into shell. Arrange cheese on top; spread remaining egg mixture over cheese. Mix yolk and water; brush lightly on edge of pastry. Invert flattened pie crust on top of filling; tuck edges under and crimp. Cut slits in top. Brush top with remaining yolk mixture. Bake in 350° oven for 50 to 55 minutes. Let stand 10 minutes. Makes 6 servings.

Meat and Potato Pie

2 *Pet-Ritz* "Deep Dish" Pie
  Crust Shells
½ cup milk
½ envelope onion soup mix
  (¼ cup)
Dash pepper
Dash ground allspice
1 pound ground beef
2 tablespoons snipped parsley
1 tablespoon butter, melted
½ teaspoon salt
1 package (12-ounce) frozen
  loose-pack hash brown potatoes, thawed (3 cups)

Remove pie crusts from freezer. Invert one crust onto waxed paper and let thaw until flattened, 10 to 15 minutes, according to directions on page 8.

In bowl combine milk, dry onion soup mix, pepper, and allspice. Add ground beef; mix thoroughly. Lightly pat meat mixture into second crust .

Combine parsley, melted butter, and salt; add thawed hash brown potatoes, stirring to coat. Spoon potatoes over meat mixture. Moisten edge of crust with a little water. Invert flattened crust on top of filling; tuck edges under and crimp. Cut slits for escape of steam.

Bake on preheated cookie sheet in 350° oven until crust is golden, about 1 hour. Makes 6 servings.

Sausage Stuffing Pie

2 *Pet-Ritz* "Deep Dish" Pie
  Crust Shells
1½ pounds pork sausage
¾ cup chopped onion
1 jar (8-ounce) *Musselman's*®
  Applesauce (1 cup)
1 cup soft bread crumbs
  (1⅓ slices)
1 teaspoon ground sage

Remove pie crusts from freezer. Invert one crust onto waxed paper and let thaw until flattened, 10 to 15 minutes, according to directions on page 8.

In skillet cook sausage and onion until meat is brown. Drain. Stir in applesauce, bread crumbs, and sage. Spoon filling into second crust in pie pan. Moisten edge of crust with water. Invert flattened crust on top of filling; tuck edge under and crimp. Cut slits in top crust. Bake on preheated cookie sheet in 375° oven 40 minutes. Makes 6 servings.

Quick Tips

Pie Crust Glazing Tips

Want to know the secret to putting that golden glow on all of your home-baked crusts? It's easy! You can use this simple trick to add rich color and flavor to any meat, fish, or poultry pie.

And, you'll want to try it on top of one crust casseroles, and meat-filled turnovers, too. Golden Egg Glaze: Combine 1 egg yolk and 1 tablespoon water; brush mixture over top of pastry before baking.

Chopped Beef Pasties

5 *Pet-Ritz* Regular Pie Crust
   Shells
1 pound beef round steak, cut in
   ¼-inch cubes
2 or 3 medium potatoes, peeled
   and coarsely chopped
   (2 cups)
1 medium turnip, peeled and cut
   in ¼-inch cubes (¾ cup)
½ cup finely chopped onion
½ cup catsup

Remove pie crusts from freezer. Invert onto waxed paper and let thaw until flattened, 10 to 15 minutes.

Combine beef, potatoes, turnip, onion, 1½ teaspoons *salt*, and ¼ teaspoon *pepper*. Spoon *about 1 cup* filling on half of each circle. Fold dough over filling to make a half-circle (see page 18). Seal edges, using tines of fork; cut slits for escape of steam. Using wide spatula transfer to ungreased baking sheets. Bake in 400° oven about 45 minutes. In small saucepan combine catsup and ¼ cup *water*; heat through. Serve sauce with pasties. Makes 5 servings.

Pizza Burger Pie

1 pound ground beef
1 medium onion, chopped
   (½ cup)
⅓ cup chopped green pepper
¾ cup water
1 can (6-ounce) tomato paste
1½ teaspoons Italian seasoning
½ teaspoon garlic powder
¼ teaspoon salt
1 *Pet-Ritz* Regular Pie Crust
   Shell
1½ cups (6 ounces) shredded
   mozzarella cheese

In a skillet cook ground beef, onion, and pepper until meat is browned. Drain off excess fat. Stir in water, tomato paste, Italian seasoning, garlic powder, and salt. Cover and simmer for 10 minutes. Spread half of the meat mixture in frozen pie crust. Sprinkle with half of the cheese. Layer remaining meat mixture and cheese. Bake in a 400° oven on preheated cookie sheet for 15 to 20 minutes. Makes 4 to 6 servings.

Bottoms Up Casserole

1 *Pet-Ritz* Regular Pie Crust
   Shell
1 pound ground beef
½ cup chopped celery
¼ cup chopped onion
¼ cup chopped green pepper
1 can (10¾-ounce) condensed
   tomato soup
½ teaspoon onion salt
⅛ teaspoon garlic powder
¾ teaspoon Worcestershire sauce
   Dash pepper
3 slices (3 ounces) American
   cheese, cut in strips

Remove pie crust from freezer. Invert onto waxed paper and let thaw until flattened, 10 to 15 minutes.

In skillet cook ground beef, celery, onion, and green pepper until meat is browned. Drain off excess fat. Stir in tomato soup, onion salt, garlic powder, Worcestershire sauce, and pepper. Spread mixture evenly in empty pie pan. Invert flattened crust on top of meat mixture; do not seal edge. Cut slits in crust for escape of steam. Place on cookie sheet and bake in 400° oven for 15 minutes. Remove pie pan from cookie sheet. Place a large plate or platter over pie; turn upside down. Remove pie pan. Top meat mixture with cheese strips in a lattice pattern. Cut in wedges. Makes 6 servings.

Puerto Rican Pork Pies

1 tablespoon cooking oil
½ pound ground pork
½ cup chopped onion
1 clove garlic, minced
¼ teaspoon dried oregano,
    crushed
¼ teaspoon dried red pepper
    flakes, crushed
½ of a 6-ounce can tomato paste
¼ cup raisins
1 tablespoon snipped parsley
1 tablespoon capers
2 teaspoons vinegar
1 hard-cooked egg, chopped
2 tablespoons chopped ripe olives
3 *Pet-Ritz* Regular Pie Crust
    Shells

Heat oil in skillet. Cook pork, onion, garlic, ½ teaspoon *salt*, oregano, red pepper, and ⅛ teaspoon *pepper* until meat is brown and onion is tender. Stir in tomato paste, raisins, parsley, capers, vinegar, and ¼ cup *water*; simmer, covered, for 5 minutes. Remove from heat. Stir in hard-cooked egg and olives.

Remove pie crusts from freezer. Invert onto waxed paper or lightly floured surface. Let thaw until flattened, 10 to 15 minutes. Roll each to a 14-inch circle, ¹⁄₁₆ inch thick. Cut each crust into fourteen 3-inch circles. Place 1 teaspoon meat mixture in the center of each circle. Fold over; moisten edges and seal well, using tines of a fork. Place on a greased baking sheet; bake in 425° oven until browned, 10 to 12 minutes. Makes 42 meat pies.

Cheeseburger Pie

1 *Pet-Ritz* "Deep Dish" Pie
    Crust Shell
½ cup *Pet* Evaporated Milk
½ cup catsup
⅓ cup fine dry bread crumbs
¼ cup chopped onion
½ teaspoon dried oregano,
    crushed
1 pound ground beef
1 cup shredded American cheese
1 teaspoon Worcestershire sauce

Prebake *unpricked* pie crust on preheated cookie sheet in 450° oven for 6 minutes, according to directions on page 6. Remove pie crust from oven. Reduce oven temperature to 350°.

In mixing bowl combine evaporated milk, catsup, bread crumbs, onion, and oregano. Add ground beef; mix well. Place meat mixture in partially baked pie crust. Bake on preheated cookie sheet in 350° oven for 35 minutes. Toss cheese with Worcestershire sauce; sprinkle on top of pie. Bake 10 minutes more. Let stand 10 minutes. Makes 6 servings.

Picnic Ham Packages

2 *Pet-Ritz* Regular Pie Crust
    Shells
1½ cups ground ham (9 ounces)
⅓ cup *Pet* Evaporated Milk
2 tablespoons catsup
2 tablespoons snipped parsley
1 teaspoon instant minced onion
1 teaspoon prepared mustard
2 hard-cooked eggs, sliced
½ cup (2 ounces) shredded Ameri-
    can cheese

Remove pie crust shells from freezer. Invert onto waxed paper and let thaw until flattened, 10 to 15 minutes.

Combine ham, milk, catsup, parsley, onion, and mustard. Cut crusts in half. Spread ¼ of the mixture on half of each piece of dough. Top with egg slices and cheese. Fold other half of dough over filling and seal edges with fork. Prick top of crust. Using wide spatula, transfer turnovers to ungreased cookie sheet. Bake in 375° oven until golden, about 25 minutes. Serve hot or chilled. Makes 4 servings.

Enticing entrées/Meat pies and pastries

Taco Pie (pictured on front cover)

1 *Pet-Ritz* "Deep Dish" Pie
  Crust Shell
1 pound ground beef
1 medium onion, chopped
  (½ cup)
1 can (15-ounce) *Old El Paso*
  Mexe-beans (Mexican chili
  beans)
1 can (6-ounce) tomato paste
1 teaspoon Worcestershire sauce
½ teaspoon chili powder
¼ teaspoon garlic powder
1½ cups corn chips
1 cup (4 ounces) shredded American cheese
  Shredded lettuce
  Tomato wedges
  Hot pepper sauce

Thaw pie crust 10 minutes. Prick bottom and sides thoroughly with tines of fork. Bake on preheated cookie sheet in 400° oven for 10 minutes, according to directions on page 6. Remove pie crust from oven; cool. Reduce oven temperature to 350°.

In skillet cook ground beef and onion until meat is browned. Drain off excess fat. Add beans, tomato paste, Worcestershire sauce, chili powder, and garlic powder. Cook and stir until mixture is heated through. Sprinkle one half of the corn chips in baked pie crust. Spoon one half of the meat mixture over chips. Repeat layers of chips and meat mixture. Bake on preheated cookie sheet in 350° oven for 30 to 35 minutes. Top with cheese, lettuce, tomatoes, and a few drops of hot pepper or taco sauce, if desired. Slice in wedges to serve. Makes 6 servings.

Reuben Pie

1 *Pet-Ritz* "Deep Dish" Pie
  Crust Shell
1 beaten egg
⅓ cup *Pet* Evaporated Milk
¾ cup soft rye bread crumbs
  (1 slice bread)
¼ cup finely chopped onion
½ teaspoon prepared mustard
¼ teaspoon salt
  Dash pepper
1 can (12-ounce) corned beef,
  flaked
8 ounces lean ground beef
1 can (8-ounce) sauerkraut, well
  drained and snipped
1 cup (4 ounces) shredded Swiss
  cheese
1 cup dairy sour cream
3 tablespoons prepared horseradish

Prebake *unpricked* pie crust on preheated cookie sheet in 450° oven for 6 minutes, according to directions on page 6. Remove pie crust from oven. Reduce oven temperature to 400°.

In mixing bowl combine milk, bread crumbs, onion, mustard, salt, and pepper. Add corned beef, ground beef, and sauerkraut. Mix well. Place half of the meat mixture in partially baked pie crust. Sprinkle one half of the cheese on top. Layer remaining meat mixture and cheese. Bake on preheated cookie sheet at 400° until crust is brown and cheese is bubbly, about 30 minutes. Let stand 10 minutes. Combine sour cream and horseradish; serve on top of pie. Makes 6 servings.

Hash Spinach Pie (pictured above)

1 *Pet-Ritz* "Deep Dish" Pie
   Crust Shell
2 packages (10 ounces each)
   frozen chopped spinach,
   cooked and drained
2 beaten eggs
1 can (10¾-ounce) condensed
   cream of mushroom soup
¼ cup all-purpose flour
1 tablespoon prepared horseradish
1 teaspoon prepared mustard
1 can (15-ounce) corned beef
   hash
1 cup shredded American cheese
2 tablespoons chopped pimiento

If desired, transfer frozen pie crust shell to ceramic or glass pie plate, according to directions on page 6. Let thaw 10 minutes. Prick bottom and sides thoroughly with tines of fork. Bake in 400° oven for 10 minutes, according to directions on page 6. Remove pie from oven. Reduce oven temperature to 350°.

Press spinach to remove excess water. Combine eggs, mushroom soup, flour, horseradish, and mustard; stir in spinach.

Spread hash in baked pastry shell; spoon spinach mixture over. Bake on preheated cookie sheet in 350° oven for 45 minutes. Sprinkle cheese and pimiento over pie. Bake 2 to 3 minutes longer. Let stand 10 minutes. Makes 6 servings.

Chicken Gumbo Casserole

1 package (10-ounce) frozen
    sliced okra, thawed
⅓ cup cooking oil
1 cup sliced green onion
1 cup finely chopped celery
½ cup chopped green pepper
1 clove garlic, minced
¼ cup all-purpose flour
1 can (13¾-ounce) chicken broth
1 can (16-ounce) tomatoes, cut up
1 *Pet-Ritz* Regular Pie Crust
    Shell
2 cups cubed cooked chicken
1 cup cooked rice

Cook okra in oil until okra appears dry, 10 to 12 minutes. Add onion, celery, green pepper, and garlic; cook 5 minutes longer, stirring occasionally. Stir in flour. Add chicken broth, *undrained* tomatoes, ½ teaspoon *salt*, ¼ teaspoon *pepper* and 1 *bay leaf*. Cook and stir until thickened and bubbly. Cover, simmer 20 minutes. Discard bay leaf.

Remove pie crust from freezer. Invert crust onto waxed paper and let thaw until flattened, 10 to 15 minutes. Add several dashes *hot pepper sauce*, chicken, and rice to okra mixture. Pour into 2-quart casserole. Invert flattened crust on top of filling. Crimp edge to lip of dish. Bake in 425° oven 20 to 25 minutes. Makes 6 servings.

Curried Chicken Salad Tarts

1 *Pet-Ritz* "Deep Dish" Pie
    Crust Shell
½ cup mayonnaise
½ cup dairy sour cream
2 tablespoons finely chopped
    chutney
½ teaspoon curry powder
2 cups chopped cooked chicken
1½ cups diced fresh pineapple
1 cup chopped celery
¼ cup slivered almonds, toasted

Remove pie crust from freezer. Invert onto waxed paper and let thaw until flattened, 10 to 15 minutes. On a lightly floured surface roll crust to a 14-inch circle. Cut into six 4½-inch rounds. Fit pastry circles over inverted muffin cups (see page 18). Prick pastry with fork. Bake in 450° oven for 7 to 10 minutes or until golden brown. Cool.

Combine mayonnaise, sour cream, chutney, and curry powder. Add chicken, pineapple, celery, and almonds. Toss lightly to coat with dressing. Spoon salad into tart shells. Chill. Makes 6 servings.

Western Casserole

⅓ cup all-purpose flour
2 to 3 teaspoons chili powder
2 teaspoons garlic salt
1½ pounds lean beef stew meat,
    cut into 1-inch cubes
3 tablespoons oil *or* shortening
1 can (10½-ounce) condensed
    beef broth
1½ cups water
1 can (16-ounce) sliced potatoes
2 packages (10 ounces each)
    frozen mixed vegetables
1 *Pet-Ritz* Regular Pie Crust
    Shell

Mix together flour, chili powder, and garlic salt. Coat meat with flour mixture. Reserve remaining flour mixture. In a large skillet brown meat half at a time in oil on all sides. Add beef broth and 1 cup of the water. Cover, simmer 1 hour until meat is nearly tender. Combine remaining flour mixture and ½ cup water. Add to meat, along with *drained* potatoes and mixed vegetables. Cook 20 minutes longer.

Meanwhile, invert frozen crust onto waxed paper. Let thaw until flattened, 10 to 15 minutes. Spoon meat mixture into 2-quart casserole. Invert flattened crust on top of filling; crimp edge to lip of dish. Cut slits in top. Bake in 425° oven 10 to 20 minutes or until crust is browned. Makes 6 servings.

Chicken Pot Pie (pictured on front cover)

2 *Pet-Ritz* "Deep Dish" Pie
   Crust Shells
2 tablespoons butter, melted
2 tablespoons all-purpose flour
¼ teaspoon dried thyme, crushed
1 cup chicken broth
¼ cup milk
2 cups cubed, cooked chicken
1 package (10-ounce) frozen peas
   and carrots, cooked and
   drained
1 medium onion, chopped

Remove pie crusts from freezer. Invert one crust onto waxed paper and let thaw until flattened, 10 to 15 minutes, according to directions on page 8.

Combine butter, flour, ½ teaspoon *salt*, thyme, and ⅛ teaspoon *pepper*. Stir in broth and milk all at once. Cook, stirring constantly, until mixture thickens and bubbles. Cook one minute more. Stir in chicken, peas and carrots, and onion. Pour into second crust in pan. Moisten edge of crust with water. Invert flattened crust on top of filling; tuck edge under and crimp. Cut slits in top. Bake on preheated cookie sheet in 425° oven until crust is brown, 35 to 40 minutes. Makes 6 servings.

Cipâte

2 large chicken breasts
1½ pounds cubed boneless pork,
   veal, and/or beef
3 tablespoons cooking oil
1 can (13¾-ounce) chicken broth
1 cup chopped onion
1 cup sliced carrot
1 cup chopped celery
1 cup chopped potato
1 cup sliced fresh mushrooms
2 tablespoons snipped parsley
1 *Pet-Ritz* Regular Pie Crust
   Shell

Remove skin and bones from chicken; cube meat. Brown meats in hot oil. Stir in broth, vegetables, parsley, 1 teaspoon *salt*, ⅛ teaspoon *pepper*, and ⅛ teaspoon *dried savory*. Cook, covered, until tender, 1¼ to 1½ hours. Remove pie crust shell from freezer. Invert onto waxed paper; thaw 10 minutes.

Meanwhile, blend ⅓ cup cold *water* into 2 tablespoons *all-purpose flour*. Stir into hot mixture. Cook and stir until thick and bubbly. Turn hot meat mixture into 2-quart casserole. Invert flattened crust on top of filling; crimp edge to lip of dish. Cut slits in top. Bake in 350° oven until golden, 30 to 35 minutes. Makes 8 to 10 servings.

Beefy Onion Pie

2 *Pet-Ritz* "Deep Dish" Pie
   Crust Shells
1½ cups thinly sliced onion
¼ cup chopped green pepper
¼ cup butter *or* margarine
2 cups chopped cooked beef
1 cup dairy sour cream
2 tablespoons all-purpose flour
¾ teaspoon salt
⅛ teaspoon pepper
1 beaten egg
2 tablespoons snipped parsley
2 tablespoons chopped pimiento

Remove pie crusts from freezer. Invert one crust onto waxed paper and let thaw until flattened, 10 to 15 minutes, according to directions on page 8.

In skillet cook onion and green pepper in butter until tender. Stir in beef; remove from heat. Combine sour cream, flour, salt, and pepper; blend in egg, parsley, and pimiento. Stir in beef mixture.

Turn beef mixture into second crust in pie pan. Moisten edge of crust with a little water. Invert flattened crust on top of filling; tuck edge under and crimp. Cut slits in top crust for escape of steam. Bake on preheated cookie sheet in 375° oven until crust is golden, about 40 minutes. Makes 6 servings.

Beef and Broccoli Pie

2 *Pet-Ritz* "Deep Dish" Pie
    Crust Shells
1 pound ground beef
¼ cup chopped onion
2 tablespoons all-purpose flour
¾ teaspoon salt
¼ teaspoon garlic salt
1¼ cups milk
1 package (3-ounce) cream
    cheese, softened
1 beaten egg
1 package (10-ounce) frozen
    chopped broccoli, cooked and
    well drained
4 ounces monterey jack cheese,
    sliced
    Milk

Remove pie crusts from freezer. Invert one crust onto waxed paper and let thaw 10 to 15 minutes, according to directions on page 8.

In a skillet brown beef and onion; drain off fat. Stir in flour, salt, and garlic salt. Add 1¼ cups milk and the softened cream cheese; cook and stir until smooth and bubbly. Stir about 1 cup of the hot mixture into the beaten egg; return to mixture in skillet. Cook and stir over medium heat until mixture is thickened, 1 to 2 minutes. Stir in cooked chopped broccoli.

Spoon the hot meat mixture into the second crust in pie pan. Arrange cheese slices on top of the meat mixture. Moisten edge of crust with a little water. Invert flattened crust on top of filling; tuck edge under and crimp. Cut slits for escape of steam.

Brush top crust with a little milk. Bake on preheated cookie sheet in 350° oven for 40 to 45 minutes. Let stand 10 minutes. Makes 6 servings.

Pigs in a Blanket

1 *Pet-Ritz* Regular *or* "Deep
    Dish" Pie Crust Shell
10 frankfurters
    Milk (optional)
    Sesame seed (optional)

Prepare pastry wedges according to directions below.

Wrap frankfurters in pastry wedges as shown in illustration. Place wrapped frankfurters, seam side down, on cookie sheet. Bake in 400° oven 15 to 20 minutes or until pastry is golden brown. Makes 10.

Variation: Prepare as above, except brush the top of each pastry wedge with a little milk and sprinkle lightly with sesame seed.

Step by step

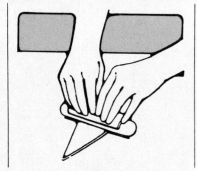

To wrap sausages in pastry wedges:

1. Remove pie crust shell from freezer. Invert frozen crust onto waxed paper or package insert. Let thaw at room temperature until pie crust flattens, about 10 to 15 minutes.

2. Roll thawed crust lightly with rolling pin until evenly flattened.

3. With sharp knife, cut pie crust in half and place one half exactly on top of other half. Cut stacked crust into five equal wedges (10 wedges in all).

4. Place one sausage across widest end of a pastry wedge; roll toward point, wrapping sausage in pastry. Repeat with remaining pastry and sausages.

5. Place pastry on cookie sheet and bake according to the recipe directions.

Sausage Roll Ups

1 *Pet-Ritz* Regular *or* "Deep Dish" Pie Crust Shell
1 package (8-ounce) fully cooked sausage links (10 sausages)

Prepare pastry wedges according to directions on page 48. Wrap sausages in pastry wedges as shown in illustration. Place wrapped sausages, seam side down, on cookie sheet. Bake in 400° oven for 15 to 20 minutes or until pastry is golden. Makes 10.

Yorkshire Christmas Meat Pie

1 1½- to 2-pound ready-to-cook rabbit
½ cup finely chopped celery
¼ cup finely chopped onion
¼ cup snipped parsley
3 tablespoons butter
3 tablespoons all-purpose flour
1 teaspoon salt
½ teaspoon ground savory
¼ teaspoon ground nutmeg
¼ teaspoon pepper
¼ teaspoon ground thyme
⅛ teaspoon ground cloves
1½ cups chicken *or* turkey broth
2 cups diced cooked chicken
2 *Pet-Ritz* "Deep Dish" Pie Crust Shells

Simmer rabbit in salted water until tender, about 1 hour. Set aside to cool. Remove cooled meat from bones; dice. In saucepan cook celery, onion, and parsley in butter until tender. Stir together flour, salt, savory, nutmeg, pepper, thyme, and cloves. Blend into celery mixture; stir in broth. Cook and stir over medium heat until mixture is thickened and bubbly. Combine mixture with rabbit and chicken.

Remove pie crusts from freezer. Invert one crust onto waxed paper and let thaw until flattened, 10 to 15 minutes, according to directions on page 8. Pour filling into second crust in pie pan. Moisten edge of crust with a little water. Invert flattened crust on top of filling; tuck edge under and crimp. Cut slits in top crust for steam to escape. Bake on preheated cookie sheet in 375° oven until golden brown, about 40 minutes. Let stand 10 minutes. Makes 6 servings.

Beef Bamboula

½ pound ground pork
1 cup finely chopped celery
¾ cup water
¼ cup chopped onion
1 teaspoon instant beef bouillon granules
1 cup milk
¼ cup all-purpose flour
2 tablespoons snipped parsley
2 tablespoons sliced ripe olives
1 tablespoon catsup
¾ teaspoon salt
¼ teaspoon pepper
2 *Pet-Ritz* "Deep Dish" Pie Crust Shells
1½ cups chopped cooked beef

Brown the pork; drain. Set aside. In saucepan combine celery, water, onion, and bouillon granules. Cover; simmer 10 minutes. Do not drain. Blend milk into flour; stir into celery mixture. Cook and stir until slightly thickened and bubbly. Stir in pork, parsley, olives, catsup, salt, and pepper. Bring to boiling; set aside.

Remove pie crust shells from freezer. Invert one crust onto waxed paper and let thaw until flattened, 10 to 15 minutes, according to directions on page 8. Spoon beef into second crust in pie pan; top with pork mixture. Moisten edge of crust with a little water. Invert flattened crust on top of filling; tuck edge under and crimp. Cut slits for escape of steam. Bake on preheated cookie sheet in 400° oven 30 to 35 minutes. Let stand 10 minutes. Makes 6 servings.

New England Clam Chowder Pie

2 *Pet-Ritz* ''Deep Dish'' Pie
    Crust Shells
2 cups chopped potato
¼ cup chopped onion
2 cans (6½ ounces each) minced
    clams
2 tablespoons butter
2 tablespoons snipped parsley
4 teaspoons all-purpose flour
¼ teaspoon salt
    Dash pepper
¾ cup milk

Remove crusts from freezer. Invert one crust onto waxed paper; let thaw 10 minutes. Cook potato and onion in 1 cup *water* until tender; drain. Drain clams, reserving liquid. Melt butter; stir in parsley, flour, ¼ teaspoon salt, and dash pepper. Add reserved clam liquid and milk; cook and stir until bubbly. Stir in potato mixture and clams. Spoon filling into second crust in pie pan. Moisten edge of crust with water. Invert flattened crust on top of filling; tuck edge under and crimp. Cut slits. Bake on preheated cookie sheet in 425° oven for 25 to 30 minutes. Let stand 10 minutes. Serves 6.

Manhattan Clam Casserole

1 *Pet-Ritz* Regular Pie Crust
    Shell
¼ cup chopped green pepper
2 tablespoons butter
2 tablespoons all-purpose flour
2 cans (10¾ ounces each)
    condensed Manhattan-style
    clam chowder
1 can (6½-ounce) minced clams
1 tablespoon minced dried onion
¼ teaspoon dried thyme, crushed
½ cup (2 ounces) shredded
    cheddar cheese
1 can (16-ounce) sliced potatoes

Remove pie crust from freezer. Invert crust onto waxed paper and let thaw 10 to 15 minutes.

In saucepan cook green pepper in butter until tender. Blend in flour. Add chowder, undrained clams, onion, and thyme. Cook and stir until mixture thickens and bubbles. Stir in cheese until melted. Drain potatoes; add to clam mixture. Turn mixture into 1½-quart casserole. Invert flattened crust on top of filling; crimp edge to lip of dish. Cut slits in top for escape of steam. Bake in 400° oven about 20 to 25 minutes or until crust is brown. Makes 6 servings.

Sour Cream-topped Clam Pie

1 *Pet-Ritz* Regular Pie Crust
    Shell
4 slices bacon
½ cup chopped onion
¼ cup all-purpose flour
¼ teaspoon salt
⅛ teaspoon pepper
    Clam liquid
1 cup drained shucked small
    clams
2 beaten eggs
2 tablespoons snipped parsley
¾ cup dairy sour cream

Prebake *unpricked* pie crust on preheated cookie sheet in 450° oven for 6 minutes. Remove pie crust from oven. Reduce temperature to 400°.

Cook bacon until crisp; remove bacon, crumble, and set aside. Cook onion in 2 tablespoons drippings until tender. Stir in flour, salt, and pepper. Add enough water to clam liquid to equal ½ cup. Add liquid and clams to skillet. Cook until thickened. Stir half the hot mixture into eggs; return to skillet. Add parsley and bacon. Spoon into partially baked pastry shell. Bake on preheated cookie sheet in 400° oven 15 minutes. Spread sour cream over top; bake until set, 4 to 5 minutes. Serves 6.

Swiss Pie with Crab Meat Sauce (pictured above)

1 *Pet-Ritz* "Deep Dish" Pie
  Crust Shell
4 slightly beaten egg yolks
1½ cups light cream
½ teaspoon salt
⅛ teaspoon ground nutmeg
4 egg whites
1½ cups (6 ounces) shredded
  natural Swiss cheese
2 tablespoons butter *or*
  margarine, melted
2 teaspoons all-purpose flour
⅛ teaspoon salt
1 cup light cream
1 can (7½-ounce) crab meat,
  drained, flaked, and cartilage
  removed

If desired, transfer frozen pie crust shell to glass or ceramic pie plate, according to directions on page 6. Prebake *unpricked* pie crust in 450° oven for 6 minutes. Remove pie crust from oven. Reduce temperature to 350°.

Combine egg yolks, 1½ cups light cream, ½ teaspoon salt, and nutmeg. Beat egg whites until stiff peaks form; fold into yolk mixture. Fold in cheese. Pour into partially baked pastry shell. Bake in 350° oven for 40 to 45 minutes or until knife inserted just off center comes out clean. Let stand 10 minutes. Serve with Crab Meat Sauce. Makes 6 servings.

Crab Meat Sauce: In saucepan blend melted butter or margarine, flour, and ⅛ teaspoon salt. Add 1 cup light cream; cook and stir until thickened and bubbly. Stir in crab meat.

51

Salmon Pie with Creamed Peas

1 *Pet-Ritz* **Regular Pie Crust Shell**
2 **beaten eggs**
½ **cup milk**
¼ **cup chopped onion**
2 **tablespoons snipped parsley**
1 **tablespoon butter, melted**
¾ **teaspoon dried basil, crushed**
¼ **teaspoon salt**
1 **can (16-ounce) salmon, drained, flaked, and cartilage removed**
1 **recipe Creamed Peas**

Remove pie crust from freezer. Invert onto waxed paper and let thaw until flattened, 10 to 15 minutes.

Meanwhile combine eggs, milk, onion, parsley, butter, basil, and salt. Add salmon; mix gently. Pour into empty pie pan. Invert flattened crust on top of filling; tuck edge under and crimp. Cut slits in top crust for steam to escape. Bake in 425° oven 25 minutes. Serve with Creamed Peas. Serves 6.

Creamed Peas: Melt 1 tablespoon *butter*; blend in 1 tablespoon *all-purpose flour*, ¼ teaspoon *salt*, and a dash *pepper*. Add 1 cup *milk* all at once. Cook and stir until bubbly. Cook and stir 2 minutes more. Stir in 1 cup cooked *peas*; heat through.

Salmon Rice Pie

2 *Pet-Ritz* **"Deep Dish" Pie Crust Shells**
½ **cup chopped onion**
2 **tablespoons butter**
1 **can (16-ounce) salmon, drained, flaked, and cartilage removed**
2 **cups cooked rice**
½ **cup milk**
2 **hard-cooked eggs, chopped**
2 **tablespoons snipped parsley**
¼ **teaspoon salt**
1 **recipe Cheese Sauce**

Remove pie crusts from freezer. Invert one crust onto waxed paper and let thaw 10 to 15 minutes.

Cook onion in butter until tender; stir in salmon, rice, milk, eggs, parsley, and salt. Spoon into second crust in pie pan. Moisten edge of crust with a little water. Invert flattened crust on top of filling; tuck edge under and crimp. Cut slits for escape of steam. Bake on preheated cookie sheet in 375° oven for 45 minutes. Serve with Cheese Sauce. Serves 6.

Cheese Sauce: Melt 2 tablespoons *butter*; blend in 2 tablespoons *all-purpose flour* and ¼ teaspoon *salt*. Add 1¼ cups *milk*; cook and stir until bubbly. Stir in ½ cup each shredded *American* and *Swiss cheese*.

Dilled Salmon Pie

1 *Pet-Ritz* **"Deep Dish" Pie Crust Shell**
2 **medium onions, chopped**
¼ **cup chopped green pepper**
2 **tablespoons butter**
1 **tablespoon snipped parsley**
¼ **teaspoon dried dillweed**
3 **tablespoons all-purpose flour**
1 **cup milk**
½ **cup shredded Swiss cheese**
1 **can (16-ounce) salmon, drained, flaked, and cartilage removed**

Prebake *unpricked* pie crust in 450° oven for 6 minutes according to directions on page 6. Remove pie crust from oven. Reduce oven to 350°.

Cook onion and green pepper in butter until tender but not brown. Stir in parsley and dillweed. Blend in flour, ½ teaspoon *salt*, and a dash *pepper*. Add milk all at once. Cook and stir until mixture thickens and bubbles. Stir in cheese until melted; fold in salmon. Pour into partially baked pastry shell. Combine ¾ cup soft *bread crumbs* and 1 tablespoon melted *butter*; sprinkle on top of pie. Bake on preheated cookie sheet in 350° oven for 30 to 35 minutes. Let stand 10 minutes. Makes 6 servings.

Fish Pie

1 *Pet-Ritz* Regular Pie Crust
Shell
2 beaten eggs
½ cup milk
1 tablespoon butter, melted
2 tablespoons chopped onion
2 tablespoons snipped parsley
2 cans (6½ or 7 ounces each)
tuna, drained and flaked

Remove pie crust from freezer. Invert onto waxed paper and let thaw until flattened, 10 to 15 minutes.

Combine eggs, milk, butter, onion, parsley, and ¼ teaspoon *salt*; stir in tuna. Pour into empty pie pan. Invert flattened crust on top of filling. Tuck edge under and crimp. Bake in 400° oven for 20 to 25 minutes. Makes 6 servings.

Shaker Fish Pie

1 *Pet-Ritz* "Deep Dish" Pie
Crust Shell
1 pound fresh *or* frozen fish
1 cup chopped onion
½ cup chopped celery
3 tablespoons butter *or*
margarine
1 tablespoon snipped parsley
½ teaspoon dried marjoram,
crushed
2 tablespoons all-purpose flour
1 teaspoon salt
Dash pepper
1 cup light cream

Prebake *unpricked* pie crust on preheated cookie sheet in 450° oven for 6 minutes, according to directions on page 6. Remove from oven; set aside. Reduce oven temperature to 325°.

Cook fish in boiling salted water to cover until fish flakes easily with a fork. Drain; break into chunks. Cook onion and celery in butter until onion is tender. Stir in parsley and marjoram. Blend in flour, salt, and pepper. Add cream; cook and stir until bubbly. Stir in fish; turn into partially baked pastry shell. Combine ⅓ cup fine dry *bread crumbs* and 2 tablespoons *butter*; sprinkle on top of pie. Bake on preheated cookie sheet in 325° oven for 30 to 35 minutes. Let stand 10 minutes. Makes 6 servings.

Tuna Cabbage Pie

2 *Pet-Ritz* "Deep Dish" Pie
Crust Shells
1 tablespoon cooking oil
2 cups chopped cabbage
1½ cups fresh sliced mushrooms
½ cup chopped onion
¼ teaspoon dried rosemary,
crushed
¼ teaspoon dried thyme, crushed
⅓ cup milk
1 package (8-ounce) cream
cheese, softened
2 hard-cooked eggs, sliced
1 can (9¼-ounce) tuna, drained
and flaked

Remove pie crusts from freezer. Invert one crust onto waxed paper and let thaw 10 minutes, according to directions on page 8.

Heat cooking oil, cabbage, mushrooms, onion, rosemary, thyme, ¼ teaspoon *salt*, and ⅛ teaspoon *pepper*. Cover; cook over low heat, stirring occasionally, for 10 minutes. Remove from heat. Blend milk into cream cheese; stir into cabbage mixture. Set aside. Arrange egg slices in bottom of second crust in pie pan; top with tuna. Spoon in cabbage mixture. Moisten edge of crust with a little water. Invert flattened crust on top of filling; tuck edge under and crimp. Cut slits in top for escape of steam. Bake on preheated cookie sheet in 375° oven 45 to 50 minutes. Makes 6 servings.

Tuna Salad Pie

1 *Pet-Ritz* "Deep Dish" Pie
Crust Shell
½ cup *Pet* Evaporated Milk
1 package (3-ounce) lemon
flavored gelatin
1 package (3-ounce) cream
cheese, cubed and softened
¼ cup mayonnaise
1 tablespoon *Musselman's* Apple
Cider Vinegar
¼ teaspoon dry mustard
1 can (9¼-ounce) tuna, drained
and flaked
2 hard-cooked eggs, chopped
⅓ cup chopped celery
¼ cup chopped green pepper
1 tablespoon grated onion

Thaw pie crust 10 minutes. Prick bottom and sides thoroughly with tines of fork. Bake on preheated cookie sheet in 400° oven for 10 minutes, according to directions on page 6. Remove pie shell from oven. Cool.

Freeze evaporated milk in small mixing bowl just until ice crystals form along edge. Dissolve gelatin in 1 cup boiling *water*. Add cream cheese; beat smooth with rotary beater. Beat in mayonnaise, vinegar, and mustard. Chill until mixture is partially set (consistency of corn syrup). Meanwhile beat evaporated milk until soft peaks form. Beat gelatin mixture until fluffy. Fold in whipped evaporated milk, tuna, eggs, celery, green pepper, and onion. Spoon into baked pie crust. Refrigerate 3 to 4 hours or until firm. Makes 6 servings.

Tuna Pot Pie

1 *Pet-Ritz* Regular Pie Crust
Shell
½ cup sliced celery
¼ cup chopped onion
1 can (9¼-ounce) tuna, drained
and flaked
1½ cups shredded cheddar cheese
1 cup frozen peas and carrots
¼ cup soft bread crumbs
¼ cup dairy sour cream
¼ cup mayonnaise
¼ cup milk
2 teaspoons prepared horseradish

Invert frozen pie crust onto waxed paper. Let thaw until flattened, 10 to 15 minutes.

In small saucepan combine celery, onion, and ¼ cup *water*; bring to boil. Reduce heat; simmer, covered, 5 minutes. Drain. Combine tuna, cheese, drained vegetables, peas and carrots, and bread crumbs. In a separate bowl combine sour cream, mayonnaise, milk, horseradish, ¼ teaspoon *salt* and a dash *pepper*. Gently stir into tuna mixture. Spoon into 1-quart casserole. Invert flattened pie crust on top of casserole; crimp edge to lip of dish. Cut slits in top. Bake in 350° oven 40 to 45 minutes or until crust is brown. Makes 4 servings.

Tuna Turnovers (pictured on back cover)

2 *Pet-Ritz* Regular Pie Crust
Shells
1 can (10-ounce) condensed
golden mushroom soup
¼ cup chopped pimiento
¼ cup chopped celery
1 can (6½- or 7-ounce) tuna,
drained
2 tablespoons dry white wine

Invert frozen pie crust onto waxed paper. Let thaw until flattened, 10 to 15 minutes. Meanwhile, combine ¼ *cup* of the soup, the pimiento, and celery. Break tuna into chunks; add to filling. Spread ½ of the filling over half of each circle to about 1 inch from edge; fold to form turnover. Seal edges; prick top. Bake on cookie sheet in 425° oven for 20 minutes. Heat remaining soup, wine, and 2 table-spoons *water*; serve with turnovers. Makes 4 servings.

Pineapple Fish Bundles (pictured above)

2 *Pet-Ritz* Regular Pie Crust
   Shells
6 breaded cooked rectangular
   fish portions
¼ cup tartar sauce
6 canned pineapple slices
3 slices (3 ounces) American
   cheese, halved

Remove pie crusts from freezer. Invert onto waxed paper and let thaw until flattened, 10 to 15 minutes. Cut each crust into 3 wedges.

Spread each fish portion with about 2 teaspoons tartar sauce; place on cookie sheet. Top each portion with 1 pineapple slice and 1 half-slice of cheese. Carefully lay one pastry wedge atop each bundle; tuck ends under. Prick top of each pastry bundle with tines of fork for escape of steam. If desired, brush with Egg Glaze according to directions on page 41. Bake in 450° oven about 15 minutes or until golden brown. Makes 6 servings.

Scallop and Artichoke Pie

1 *Pet-Ritz* Regular Pie Crust
  Shell
1 package (12-ounce) frozen
  scallops, thawed
½ cup chicken broth
¼ cup dry white wine
  Milk
2 tablespoons sliced green onion
3 tablespoons butter *or*
  margarine
3 tablespoons all-purpose flour
¼ teaspoon salt
¼ teaspoon dried thyme, crushed
  Dash pepper
½ cup (2 ounces) shredded
  gruyére cheese,
1 package (10-ounce) frozen
  artichoke hearts, cooked and
  drained
1 slightly beaten egg
1 tablespoon water

Remove pie crust from freezer. Invert onto waxed paper and let thaw until flattened, 10 to 15 minutes.

Cut large scallops in half. In small covered saucepan, simmer scallops in broth and wine until done, about 4 minutes. Drain, reserving liquid. Add milk to liquid to make 2 cups. Set aside. In medium saucepan cook onion in butter or margarine until tender but not brown. Stir in flour, salt, thyme, and pepper. Add milk mixture all at once. Cook and stir until mixture thickens and bubbles. Add cheese, stirring until melted. Stir in scallops and artichokes. Pour into 1½-quart casserole. Invert flattened crust on top of filling; crimp edge to lip of dish. Cut slits in top for steam to escape. Brush with mixture of beaten egg and water. Bake in 450° oven about 20 minutes or until crust is brown. Makes 4 servings.

Shrimp Creole Casserole

1 *Pet-Ritz* Regular Pie Crust
  Shell
½ cup chopped onion
½ cup chopped celery
½ cup chopped green pepper
1 clove garlic, minced
2 tablespoons butter *or*
  margarine
1 can (16-ounce) tomatoes, cut up
1 can (8-ounce) tomato sauce
1 tablespoon Worcestershire
  sauce
1 teaspoon salt
½ teaspoon dried thyme, crushed
2 tablespoons water
1 tablespoon cornstarch
12 ounces fresh *or* frozen shelled
  shrimp, thawed and deveined
1 cup cooked rice

Remove pie crust from freezer. Invert onto waxed paper and let thaw until flattened, 10 to 15 minutes.

Cook onion, celery, green pepper, and garlic in butter or margarine until tender but not brown. Add *undrained* tomatoes, tomato sauce, Worcestershire, salt, and thyme. Cover and simmer 10 minutes. Blend water and cornstarch. Add to tomato mixture; cook and stir until mixture thickens and bubbles. Stir in shrimp and rice. Pour into 1½-quart casserole. Invert flattened crust on top of filling; crimp edge to lip of dish. Cut slits in top for escape of steam. Bake in 425° oven 20 to 25 minutes or until crust is brown. Makes 4 servings.

Paella Pot Pie

1 *Pet-Ritz* Regular Pie Crust
   Shell
2 slices bacon
½ cup chopped onion
¼ cup chopped green pepper
1 tablespoon cornstarch
1 can (8-ounce) tomatoes, cut up
1 cup chicken broth
⅛ teaspoon pepper
⅛ teaspoon saffron, crushed
1 can (7½-ounce) minced clams
1 can (4½-ounce) shrimp
1 cup diced cooked chicken

Remove pie crust from freezer. Invert onto waxed paper and let thaw until flattened, 10 to 15 minutes.

In skillet cook bacon until crisp; crumble and set aside. Cook onion and green pepper in bacon drippings until tender but not brown. Stir in cornstarch. Add *undrained* tomatoes, broth, pepper, and saffron. Cook and stir until mixture thickens and bubbles. Drain clams and shrimp. Stir clams, shrimp, chicken, and crumbled bacon into skillet. Pour mixture into 1-quart casserole. Invert flattened crust on top of filling; crimp edge to lip of dish. Cut slits for escape of steam. Bake in 450° oven 20 minutes. Makes 4 servings.

Oyster Pie Hangtown

1 *Pet-Ritz* Regular Pie Crust
   Shell
1 pint oysters, undrained
6 beaten eggs
¼ cup milk *or* cream
1 tablespoon snipped parsley
¼ teaspoon salt
   Dash pepper
2 tablespoons butter
⅓ cup fine dry bread crumbs
¼ teaspoon paprika
1 tablespoon butter, melted

Thaw pie crust 10 minutes. Prick bottom and sides with fork. Bake on preheated cookie sheet in 400° oven for 10 minutes (see page 6).

Cook *undrained* oysters until edges curl, about 3 minutes. Drain and set aside. Combine eggs, milk, parsley, salt, and pepper. In skillet melt the 2 tablespoons butter. Add egg mixture and scramble until eggs are set but still shiny. Spread eggs in bottom of baked pie crust. Arrange oysters over top. Sprinkle with salt and pepper. Combine bread crumbs, paprika, and remaining butter; sprinkle on top of oysters. Bake in 400° oven for 10 minutes. Makes 6 servings.

Egg Foo Yung Pie

1 *Pet-Ritz* Regular Pie Crust
   Shell
½ cup sliced celery
¼ cup sliced green onion
¼ cup chopped green pepper
1 tablespoon cooking oil
1 can (4½-ounce) shrimp
1 cup bean sprouts
¼ cup chopped water chestnuts
6 slightly beaten eggs
1 cup chicken broth
2 teaspoons soy sauce
4 teaspoons cornstarch

Prebake *unpricked* pie crust on preheated cookie sheet in 450° oven for 6 minutes (see page 6). Remove from oven. Reduce temperature to 350°.

Cook celery, onion, and pepper in oil until tender, about 5 minutes. Remove from heat. Stir in shrimp, bean sprouts, water chestnuts, and eggs. Pour into partially baked pastry shell. Bake on preheated cookie sheet in 350° oven until set, about 30 minutes. Let stand 10 minutes. Meanwhile, in small saucepan combine chicken broth, soy sauce, and cornstarch. Cook and stir until bubbly. Serve over pie wedges. Makes 6 servings.

Pies and pastries for a perfect ending

Serving delicious cream pies, smooth rich custards, or warm-from-the-oven fruit-filled turnovers and dumplings is a surefire way to please the pastry-lovers around your house. Each luscious-tasting recipe begins with a convenient *Pet-Ritz* pie crust shell and ends as a perfect dessert for any occasion.

For starters, tempt your family with this tried, true, and traditional Lemon Meringue Pie. You'll find the recipe on page 68.

Pumpkin Apple Pie (pictured right, front)

1 *Pet-Ritz* "Deep Dish" Pie
    Crust Shell
½ cup packed brown sugar
½ cup water
2 tablespoons butter
1 tablespoon cornstarch
1 teaspoon ground cinnamon
¼ teaspoon salt
4 cups sliced, peeled cooking
    apples
1 tablespoon lemon juice
1 slightly beaten egg
1 cup canned pumpkin
½ cup granulated sugar
½ teaspoon ground ginger
⅛ teaspoon ground cloves
¼ teaspoon salt
1 small can (5.33 fl. oz.) *Pet*
    Evaporated Milk

If desired, transfer frozen pie shell to glass or ceramic pie plate, according to directions on page 6. Prebake *unpricked* pie crust in 450° oven for 6 minutes. Remove from oven. Reduce temperature to 375°.

In medium saucepan combine brown sugar, water, butter, cornstarch, cinnamon, and ¼ teaspoon salt. Cook and stir over medium heat until mixture comes to boiling. Stir in sliced apples. Cover and cook for 5 to 6 minutes or until apples are crisp-tender, stirring occasionally. Remove from heat; stir in lemon juice. Spread apple mixture in bottom of partially baked pie crust.

In mixing bowl combine egg, pumpkin, granulated sugar, ginger, cloves, and the remaining ¼ teaspoon salt; mix well. Stir in evaporated milk. Carefully pour pumpkin mixture over apple layer. Bake in 375° oven for 40 to 45 minutes or until knife inserted off center comes out clean. Cool pie thoroughly on rack. Serve with *Pet Whip*, if desired.

Fig Nut Pie (pictured right, back)

1 *Pet-Ritz* "Deep Dish" Pie
    Crust Shell
6 beaten eggs
1 cup sugar
3 tablespoons lemon juice
3 tablespoons butter, melted
½ teaspoon ground cinnamon
½ teaspoon ground nutmeg
1½ cups chopped dried figs
1 cup chopped *Funsten* Walnuts

If desired, transfer frozen pie shell to glass or ceramic pie plate, according to directions on page 6. Prebake *unpricked* pie crust in 450° oven for 6 minutes. Remove pie crust from oven. Reduce oven temperature to 375°.

In mixing bowl combine eggs, sugar, lemon juice, butter, cinnamon, nutmeg, and ¼ teaspoon *salt*. Stir in figs and walnuts. Pour filling into partially baked pie crust. Bake in 375° oven for 40 minutes, or until knife inserted off center comes out clean. Cool.

Caramel Custard Pie

1 *Pet-Ritz* "Deep Dish" Pie
    Crust Shell
2 eggs, slightly beaten
1 tall can (13 fl. oz.) *Pet*
    Evaporated Milk
⅔ cup water
1 cup packed brown sugar
3 tablespoons all-purpose flour
2 tablespoons butter

Prebake *unpricked* pie crust shell on preheated cookie sheet in 450° oven for 6 minutes (see page 6). Remove from oven. Reduce temperature to 400°.

Combine eggs, evaporated milk, and water. Combine brown sugar and flour; cut in butter until crumbly. Add milk mixture; beat well. Pour into partially baked pie shell. Bake on preheated cookie sheet in 400° oven for 30 minutes or until knife inserted just off center comes out clean. Cool.

Nutty Raisin Pie

1 *Pet-Ritz* **Regular Pie Crust**
   Shell
¼ **cup butter** *or* **margarine**
¾ **cup sugar**
 2 **slightly beaten eggs**
½ **cup raisins**
½ **cup shredded coconut**
½ **cup chopped** *Funsten* **Pecans**
 1 **teaspoon vanilla**
   Pet Whip **Non-Dairy Whipped**
   Topping, thawed

Prebake *unpricked* pie crust shell on preheated cookie sheet in 450° oven for 6 minutes, according to directions on page 6. Remove pie crust from oven. Reduce oven temperature to 350°.

In mixing bowl stir together butter or margarine and sugar. Add eggs and mix well. Stir in raisins, coconut, pecans, and vanilla. Pour into partially baked pastry shell. Bake on preheated cookie sheet in 350° oven for 30 to 35 minutes or until mixture is set. Serve warm or cool. Garnish with *Pet Whip*, if desired.

Rhubarb Custard Pie

1 *Pet-Ritz* "Deep Dish" Pie
   Crust Shell
1 cup sugar
3 tablespoons all-purpose flour
¼ teaspoon salt
3 egg yolks
3 tablespoons frozen orange juice
   concentrate
2 tablespoons butter, softened
3 cups fresh rhubarb *or* one
   package (13-ounce) frozen
   unsweetened rhubarb, cut in
   ½-inch pieces
3 egg whites
⅓ cup sugar
⅓ cup chopped *Funsten* Pecans

Prebake *unpricked* pie crust shell on preheated cookie sheet in 450° oven for 6 minutes, according to directions on page 6. Remove pie shell from oven. Reduce oven temperature to 325°.

Combine the 1 cup sugar, the flour, and salt. Add egg yolks, juice concentrate, and butter; beat smooth with rotary beater. Stir in rhubarb. Beat egg whites to soft peaks (tips curl over). Gradually add the ⅓ cup sugar, beating to stiff peaks (tips stand straight). Gently fold whites into rhubarb mixture. Pour into partially baked pie crust; sprinkle with nuts. Bake on a preheated cookie sheet in 325° oven 55 minutes. Cool on wire rack.

Maple Syrup Pie

1 *Pet-Ritz* "Deep Dish" Pie
   Crust Shell
3 slightly beaten eggs
1 cup pure maple syrup
½ cup packed brown sugar
2 tablespoons butter *or* margarine, melted
2 tablespoons all-purpose flour
1 teaspoon vanilla
   Dash salt
½ cup chopped *Funsten* Pecans

Prebake *unpricked* pie crust shell on preheated cookie sheet in 450° oven for 6 minutes, according to directions on page 6. Remove pie shell from oven. Reduce oven temperature to 350°.

In mixing bowl combine eggs, syrup, sugar, butter or margarine, flour, vanilla, and salt. Beat smooth with rotary beater. Stir in nuts. Turn mixture into partially baked pie crust. Bake on preheated cookie sheet in 350° oven about 40 minutes, or till knife inserted off center comes out clean. Cool on wire rack.

Coconut Pecan Pie

1 *Pet-Ritz* "Deep Dish" Pie
   Crust Shell
3 beaten eggs
1½ cups sugar
¼ cup butter *or* margarine,
   melted
2 tablespoons orange juice
1 teaspoon vanilla
1 to 1½ cups coarsely chopped
   Funsten Pecans
½ cup flaked coconut

Prebake *unpricked* pie crust on preheated cookie sheet in 450° oven for 6 minutes, according to directions on page 6. Remove pie crust from oven. Reduce oven temperature to 350°.

Combine eggs, sugar, butter or margarine, orange juice, and vanilla; stir in nuts and coconut. Pour egg mixture into partially baked pie crust. Bake on preheated cookie sheet in 350° oven for 40 to 45 minutes or until knife inserted just off center comes out clean. Serve warm or cool.

Brownie Scotch Pie

1 *Pet-Ritz* "Deep Dish" Pie
    Crust Shell
1½ cups packed brown sugar
¼ cup butter *or* margarine
3 eggs
1 1-ounce square unsweetened
    chocolate, melted and cooled
½ cup milk
1 teaspoon vanilla

Prebake *unpricked* pie crust on preheated cookie sheet in 450° oven for 6 minutes, according to directions on page 6. Remove pie crust from oven. Reduce oven temperature to 375°.

In mixer bowl beat brown sugar and butter or margarine with electric mixer or rotary beater until well combined. Add eggs, one at a time, beating at low speed just until combined. Blend in cooled chocolate; stir in milk and vanilla. (Mixture may look slightly curdled.) Pour filling into partially baked pie shell. Bake on preheated cookie sheet in 375° oven for 30 to 35 minutes or until knife inserted off center comes out clean. Cool.

Fresh Peach Custard Pie

1 *Pet-Ritz* "Deep Dish" Pie
    Crust Shell
3 cups sliced fresh *or* frozen
    peaches
⅔ cup sugar
2 tablespoons all-purpose flour
¼ teaspoon salt
2 slightly beaten eggs
1 cup light cream *or* milk
    Ground nutmeg

Prebake *unpricked* pie crust shell on preheated cookie sheet in 450° oven for 6 minutes, according to directions on page 6. Remove pie shell from oven. Reduce oven temperature to 350°. Thaw peaches, if frozen; drain and thinly slice.

Place sliced peaches in bottom of partially baked pastry shell. Combine sugar, flour, and salt; stir in eggs. Stir in light cream or milk; pour over peaches. Sprinkle with nutmeg. Bake on preheated cookie sheet in 350° oven for 45 to 50 minutes, or until knife inserted off center comes out clean. Cool on rack before serving.

Lemon Chess Pie

1 *Pet-Ritz* "Deep Dish" Pie
    Crust Shell
5 eggs
1½ cups sugar
1 cup light cream *or* milk
¼ cup butter *or* margarine,
    melted
1 teaspoon finely shredded lemon
    peel
2 tablespoons lemon juice
1 tablespoon all-purpose flour
1 tablespoon yellow cornmeal
1½ teaspoons vanilla

Prebake *unpricked* pie crust shell on preheated cookie sheet in 450° oven for 6 minutes, according to directions on page 6. Remove pie crust from oven. Reduce oven temperature to 350°.

In medium mixing bowl beat eggs until well blended. Stir in sugar, light cream or milk, melted butter or margarine, shredded lemon peel, lemon juice, flour, cornmeal, and vanilla. Mix well.

Pour filling into the partially baked pastry shell. To prevent over-browning, cover edge of pie with foil. Bake on preheated cookie sheet in 350° oven for 20 minutes. Remove foil; bake for 20 to 25 minutes more or until knife inserted off center comes out clean. Cool pie on rack before serving.

Chocolate Crunch Pie

1 *Pet-Ritz* "Deep Dish" Pie
   Crust Shell
4 slightly beaten eggs
1 cup packed brown sugar
1 cup dark corn syrup
2 tablespoons butter *or* margarine, melted
1 teaspoon vanilla
1 cup peanuts
½ cup semisweet chocolate pieces
   Pet Whip Non-Dairy Whipped
   Topping, thawed

Prebake *unpricked* pie crust shell on preheated cookie sheet in 450° oven for 6 minutes, according to directions on page 6. Remove pie crust from oven. Reduce oven temperature to 350°.

In mixing bowl combine eggs, sugar, corn syrup, butter or margarine, and vanilla. Add peanuts and chocolate pieces. Pour into partially baked pastry shell. Bake on preheated cookie sheet in 350° oven for 35 to 45 minutes or until knife inserted just off center comes out clean. Cool on wire rack. Garnish with dollops of *Pet Whip*.

Coconut Custard Pie

1 *Pet-Ritz* "Deep Dish" Pie
   Crust Shell
½ cup sugar
¼ cup butter *or* margarine,
   softened
1 cup dark *or* light corn syrup
¼ teaspoon salt
3 well-beaten eggs
½ cup shredded coconut
½ cup quick-cooking rolled oats

Prebake *unpricked* pie crust shell on preheated cookie sheet in 450° oven for 6 minutes, according to directions on page 6. Remove pie crust from oven. Reduce oven temperature to 350°.

In mixer bowl cream together sugar and butter or margarine on medium speed of electric mixer until light and fluffy. Add syrup and salt; beat well. Beat in eggs, one at a time. Stir in coconut and oats. Pour into partially baked pie crust. Bake on preheated cookie sheet in 350° oven 50 minutes or until knife inserted off center comes out clean. Cool on wire rack.

Pumpkin Pie

1 *Pet-Ritz* "Deep Dish" Pie
   Crust Shell
1 can (16-ounce) pumpkin
¾ cup sugar
1 teaspoon ground cinnamon
½ teaspoon salt
½ teaspoon ground ginger
½ teaspoon ground nutmeg
3 eggs
1 small can (5.33 fl. oz.) *Pet*
   Evaporated Milk
½ cup milk
   Pet Whip Non-Dairy Whipped
   Topping, thawed

Prebake *unpricked* pie crust shell on preheated cookie sheet in 450° oven for 6 minutes, according to directions on page 6. Remove pie crust from oven. Reduce oven temperature to 375°.

In large mixing bowl combine pumpkin, sugar, cinnamon, salt, ginger, and nutmeg. Add eggs; beat with a fork. Add the evaporated milk and milk; mix well. Pour mixture into partially baked pastry shell. Bake on preheated cookie sheet in 375° oven for 50 to 55 minutes or until knife inserted off center comes out clean. Cool on rack before serving. Garnish with dollops of *Pet Whip*.

Custard Pie

1 *Pet-Ritz* "Deep Dish" Pie
   Crust shell
4 eggs
½ cup sugar
½ teaspoon vanilla
¼ teaspoon salt
2½ cups milk
   Ground nutmeg

Prebake *unpricked* pie crust shell on preheated cookie sheet in 450° oven for 6 minutes, according to directions on page 6. Remove pie crust from oven. Reduce oven temperature to 350°.

In mixing bowl beat eggs slightly with rotary beater or fork. Stir in the sugar, vanilla, and salt. Gradually stir in milk; mix well. Pour filling into partially baked pastry shell. Sprinkle with a little nutmeg. Bake on preheated cookie sheet in 350° oven for 60 minutes or until knife inserted off center comes out clean. Cool pie on rack before serving.

Pecan Tassies

2 *Pet-Ritz* "Deep Dish" Pie
   Crust Shells
1 beaten egg
¾ cup packed brown sugar
1 tablespoon butter *or*
   margarine, softened
1 teaspoon vanilla
   Dash salt
½ cup coarsely chopped *Funsten*
   Pecans

Remove pie crust shells from freezer. Invert onto waxed paper and let thaw 10 to 15 minutes, according to directions on page 6. Roll each thawed crust lightly with rolling pin to smooth and flatten. Cut each into twelve 2½-inch circles. Fit pastry circles into twenty-four 1¾-inch muffin cups, according to directions on page 18.

In small mixing bowl stir together egg, brown sugar, butter or margarine, vanilla, and salt just until smooth. Spoon about 1 teaspoon of the chopped pecans into *each* pastry-lined muffin cup; fill each with egg mixture. Bake in 325° oven about 25 minutes or until filling is set. Cool; remove from pans. Makes 24.

Pecan Pie

1 *Pet-Ritz* "Deep Dish" Pie
   Crust Shell
3 eggs
⅔ cup sugar
   Dash salt
1 cup dark corn syrup
⅓ cup butter *or* margarine,
   melted
1 cup *Funsten* Pecan Halves
   Vanilla ice cream

Prebake *unpricked* pie crust shell on preheated cookie sheet in 450° oven for 6 minutes, according to directions on page 6. Remove pie crust from oven. Reduce oven temperature to 350°.

In mixing bowl beat eggs slightly with rotary beater or fork. Add sugar and salt, stirring until dissolved. Stir in dark corn syrup and melted butter or margarine; mix well. Stir in the pecan halves. Pour filling into partially baked pastry shell. Bake on preheated cookie sheet in 350° oven for 50 minutes or until knife inserted off center comes out clean. Cool on rack before serving. Serve with vanilla ice cream, if desired.

Chocolate Almond Marble Pie (pictured above)

6 tablespoons milk
¼ cup almond paste
2 1-ounce squares semisweet chocolate, melted and cooled
1 package (4½- or 5⅝-ounce) *regular* vanilla pudding mix
1 *Pet-Ritz* Graham Cracker Crust

In small mixer bowl add 1 tablespoon of the milk at a time to almond paste, beating with electric mixer or rotary beater until smooth. Add the chocolate, beating until well blended. Set aside.

In saucepan prepare vanilla pudding mix according to package directions for pie filling. Cool pudding mixture 5 minutes, stirring gently twice. Spread 1 cup of the warm pudding mixture over bottom of graham cracker crust. Dot with half of the chocolate mixture. Spread remaining pudding mixture on top; dot with remaining chocolate mixture.

With narrow spatula, swirl gently through pie to marble. Cover; chill several hours or until firm.

Lemon Layer Date Pie

1 *Pet-Ritz* "Deep Dish" Pie
   Crust Shell
1 cup (8 ounces) snipped pitted
   dates
¼ cup honey
¼ cup water
1 tablespoon lemon juice
⅓ cup chopped *Funsten* Walnuts
1 package (3-ounce) *regular*
   lemon pudding mix
⅓ cup sugar
2¼ cups water
1 beaten egg
   Pet Whip Non-Dairy Whipped
   Topping, thawed

Thaw pie crust 10 minutes. Prick bottom and sides thoroughly with tines of fork. Bake on preheated cookie sheet in 400° oven for 10 minutes, according to directions on page 6. Remove pie crust from oven.

In saucepan combine dates, honey, the ¼ cup water, and the lemon juice. Bring to a boil. Reduce heat; simmer 10 minutes, stirring often. Add nuts; cool. Pour into pie crust.

In saucepan combine pudding mix and sugar; stir in the 2¼ cups water. Add egg. Cook and stir until thickened and bubbly; cook 2 minutes more. Cover with waxed paper; cool. Pour cooled pudding over date mixture in pie crust. Cool. Spread *Pet Whip* evenly over top of pie. Chill until serving time.

Spiced Butterscotch Pie

1 *Pet-Ritz* Regular Pie Crust
   Shell
¼ cup finely chopped *Funsten*
   Walnuts
½ teaspoon ground cinnamon
¼ teaspoon ground nutmeg
   Dash ground ginger
1 package (3⅝-ounce) *regular*
   butterscotch pudding mix
   Pet Whip Non-Dairy Whipped
   Topping, thawed

Thaw pie crust 10 minutes. Sprinkle with chopped walnuts. Press nuts gently into crust. Prick bottom and sides thoroughly with tines of fork. Bake on preheated cookie sheet in 400° oven for 10 minutes (see page 6). Remove pie crust from oven. Cool.

Add spices to dry pudding mix; cook according to package directions. Cool 5 minutes; pour into baked pastry shell. Cover surface of pudding with waxed paper. Chill. To serve, remove waxed paper from pie; spread whipped topping evenly over butterscotch filling.

Black Bottom Butterscotch Pie

1 *Pet-Ritz* "Deep Dish" Pie
   Crust Shell
⅓ cup semisweet chocolate pieces
¾ cup packed brown sugar
3 tablespoons cornstarch
¼ teaspoon salt
2 cups milk
3 slightly beaten egg yolks
3 tablespoons butter *or*
   margarine
1 teaspoon vanilla

Thaw pie crust 10 minutes. Prick bottom and sides thoroughly with tines of fork. Bake on preheated cookie sheet in 400° oven for 10 minutes. Sprinkle chocolate pieces on crust. Return to oven for 1 to 2 minutes. Spread melted chips over bottom and sides of pie shell. Cool.

In saucepan combine sugar, cornstarch, and salt. Add milk. Cook and stir until bubbly. Cook and stir 2 minutes more. Remove from heat. Stir half the hot mixture into beaten yolks; return to hot mixture in saucepan. Cook 2 minutes, stirring constantly. Remove from heat. Add butter and vanilla. Cover surface; cool completely. Pour filling into pie shell.

Lemon Meringue Pie (pictured on pages 58 and 59)

1 *Pet-Ritz* "Deep Dish" Pie
   Crust Shell
1½ cups sugar
  3 tablespoons cornstarch
  3 tablespoons all-purpose flour
   Dash salt
1½ cups water
  3 eggs, separated
  2 tablespoons butter *or*
   margarine
½ teaspoon finely shredded lemon
   peel
⅓ cup lemon juice
½ teaspoon vanilla
¼ teaspoon cream of tartar
  6 tablespoons sugar

Thaw pie crust 10 minutes. Prick bottom and sides thoroughly with tines of fork. Bake in 400° oven for 10 minutes, according to directions on page 6. Remove pie crust from oven; cool.

In medium saucepan combine the 1½ cups sugar, cornstarch, flour, and salt. Gradually stir in water. Cook and stir over medium high heat until thickened and bubbly. Reduce heat; cook 2 minutes more. Remove from heat. Beat egg yolks slightly. Stir about 1 cup of the hot mixture into the beaten yolks. Return mixture to saucepan; cook and stir 2 minutes more. Remove from heat. Stir in butter or margarine and lemon peel. Gradually stir in lemon juice, mixing well. Pour filling into baked pie crust. Spread Meringue on top of hot filling, sealing to edges of pastry. Bake in 350° oven for 12 to 15 minutes. Cool; chill.

Meringue: In mixer bowl beat egg whites, vanilla, and cream of tartar till soft peaks form (tips curl over). Gradually add the 6 tablespoons sugar, beating to stiff peaks (tips stand straight).

Elegant Strawberry Pie

1 *Pet-Ritz* "Deep Dish" Pie
   Crust Shell
¼ cup sugar
  2 tablespoons cornstarch
⅓ cup water
⅓ cup grenadine syrup
  1 tablespoon lemon juice
⅓ cup sliced *Funsten* Almonds,
   toasted
  1 package (3½-ounce) *instant*
   vanilla pudding mix
1¼ cups milk
  1 cup dairy sour cream
  2 cups sliced fresh strawberries

Thaw pie crust 10 minutes. Prick bottom and sides thoroughly with tines of fork. Bake on preheated cookie sheet in 400° oven for 10 minutes, according to directions on page 6. Remove pie crust from oven; cool.

To make berry glaze: Combine sugar and cornstarch. Blend in water, grenadine syrup, and lemon juice. Cook and stir over medium heat until mixture thickens and bubbles. Cover and cool at room temperature (do not chill). Sprinkle almonds on bottom of pie crust; set aside.

For filling: In small mixer bowl combine pudding mix, milk, and sour cream. Beat at low speed on electric mixer about 1 minute, using a rubber spatula to guide mixture toward beaters. Immediately pour pudding over almonds in pie crust. Spread one-third of the berry glaze on top of filling. Arrange the sliced strawberries on top in a circular pattern, beginning next to crust. Spoon remaining berry glaze over fruit. Chill until serving time.

Peanut Butter Pie

2 packages (3 ounces each) cream
  cheese, softened
¾ cup sifted powdered sugar
½ cup peanut butter
2 tablespoons milk
2 cups *Pet Whip* Non-Dairy
  Whipped Topping, thawed
1 *Pet-Ritz* Graham Cracker Crust
  Chopped peanuts

In small mixer bowl beat together cream cheese and sugar until light and fluffy. Add peanut butter and milk, beating until smooth and creamy. Fold *Pet Whip* into peanut butter mixture. Turn into graham cracker crust. Chill 5 to 6 hours or overnight. Garnish top with coarsely chopped peanuts.

Chocolate Cream Pie

1 *Pet-Ritz* Regular Pie Crust
  Shell
1 cup sugar
3 tablespoons cornstarch
¼ teaspoon salt
2 cups milk
2 1-ounce squares unsweetened
  chocolate, chopped
3 eggs, separated
2 tablespoons butter
1 teaspoon vanilla
½ teaspoon vanilla
¼ teaspoon cream of tartar
6 tablespoons sugar

Thaw pie crust 10 minutes. Prick bottom and sides thoroughly with tines of fork. Bake on preheated cookie sheet in 400° oven for 10 minutes, according to directions on page 6. Remove pie from oven; cool.

In saucepan combine the 1 cup sugar, cornstarch, and salt; gradually stir in milk. Add chocolate. Cook and stir over medium high heat until bubbly. Cook and stir 2 minutes. Remove from heat. Stir about 1 cup of the hot mixture into yolks; immediately return to hot mixture. Cook 2 minutes, stirring constantly. Remove from heat. Add butter and 1 teaspoon vanilla. Pour into baked pastry shell. Spread Meringue on top of filling; bake in 350° oven 12 to 15 minutes.

Meringue: In mixer bowl beat egg whites, vanilla, and cream of tartar until soft peaks form. Gradually add the 6 tablespoons sugar, beating to stiff peaks.

Chocolate Silk Pie

1 *Pet-Ritz* Regular Pie Crust
  Shell
½ cup butter *or* margarine,
  softened
¾ cup sugar
2 1-ounce squares unsweetened
  chocolate, melted and cooled
1 teaspoon vanilla
2 eggs
1½ cups *Pet Whip* Non-Dairy
  Whipped Topping, thawed
2 tablespoons finely chopped
  Funsten Pecans

Thaw pie crust 10 minutes. Prick bottom and sides thoroughly with tines of fork. Bake on preheated cookie sheet in 400° oven for 10 minutes, according to directions on page 6. Remove pie crust from oven; cool. Beat butter or margarine until smooth and creamy. Gradually beat in sugar until fluffy. Blend in chocolate and vanilla. Add eggs, one at a time, beating 3 minutes after each addition.

Pour filling in baked pie shell. Chill several hours or until set. Just before serving, spread whipped topping over chilled filling. Sprinkle pecans over pie.

Lemon Sour Cream Tarts

2 *Pet-Ritz* "Deep Dish" Pie
    Crust Shells
1 can (18-ounce) lemon pudding
1 cup dairy sour cream
1 package (10-ounce) frozen
    raspberries, thawed
2 tablespoons sugar
1 tablespoon cornstarch

Remove pie crust shells from freezer. Invert frozen crusts onto waxed paper or insert. Let thaw until crusts flatten, 10 to 15 minutes. Roll each thawed crust to a 14-inch circle, 1/16 inch thick. Cut each circle into six 4½-inch rounds. Fit pastry circles over inverted muffin cups, according to directions on page 18. Prick pastry. Bake in 450° oven for 7 to 10 minutes. Let cool slightly; lift off muffin cup. Cool completely right side up on wire rack.

Combine lemon pudding and sour cream; chill. Drain raspberries, reserving ⅔ cup syrup. In small saucepan combine sugar and cornstarch; blend in reserved syrup. Cook and stir over medium heat until thickened and bubbly. Cover with waxed paper and chill.

To assemble tarts, spoon lemon mixture into baked tart shells; top with a few berries. Spoon about 1 tablespoon raspberry glaze over raspberries in tart shells. Serve chilled. Makes 12 tarts.

Banana Apricot Pie

1 *Pet-Ritz* "Deep Dish" Pie
    Crust Shell
2 cups dried apricots, snipped
1½ cups water
1¼ cups sugar
¼ cup all-purpose flour
¼ teaspoon salt
3 eggs, separated
2 tablespoons butter *or* marga-
    rine
2 medium bananas, thinly sliced
½ teaspoon vanilla
¼ teaspoon cream of tartar
6 tablespoons sugar

Thaw pie crust 10 minutes. Prick bottom and sides thoroughly with tines of fork. Bake on preheated cookie sheet in 400° oven for 10 minutes, according to directions on page 6. Remove pie crust from oven; cool.

In saucepan combine apricots and water. Cover and simmer 10 minutes or until tender. Combine 1¼ cups sugar, flour, and salt; stir into apricot mixture. Cook and stir until thickened and bubbly. Reduce heat; cook and stir 2 minutes more. Remove from heat. Beat egg yolks slightly. Gradually stir 1 cup of the hot mixture into yolks. Return mixture to saucepan; cook and stir 2 minutes more. Remove from heat. Stir in butter. Arrange bananas in baked pastry shell; pour apricot mixture on top. Spread Meringue over hot filling; seal to edge. Bake in 350° oven for 12 to 15 minutes. Cool on wire rack.

Meringue: Beat egg whites, vanilla, and cream of tartar until soft peaks form (tips curl over). Gradually add 6 tablespoons sugar, beating until stiff peaks form (tips stand straight).

Upside-Down Chocolate Pie

1 *Pet-Ritz* "Deep Dish" Pie
   Crust Shell
3 eggs, separated
½ teaspoon vinegar
¼ teaspoon ground cinnamon
½ cup sugar
1 package (6-ounce) semisweet
   chocolate pieces (1 cup)
¼ cup water
1½ cups whipping cream
¼ cup sugar

Thaw pie crust 10 minutes. Prick bottom and sides thoroughly with tines of fork. Bake on preheated cookie sheet in 400° oven for 10 minutes, according to directions on page 6. Remove pie from oven; cool.

In small mixer bowl combine egg whites, vinegar, and cinnamon. Beat with electric mixer to soft peaks (tips curl over). Gradually add the ½ cup sugar, beating to stiff peaks (tips stand straight). Spread over the bottom and up the sides of the baked pie crust. Bake in a 325° oven for 15 minutes. Remove from oven and cool on rack.

Melt chocolate in a saucepan over low heat; cool to room temperature. In a bowl beat together egg yolks and water till blended. Gradually stir in the melted and cooled chocolate. Spread ¼ cup of the chocolate mixture over the meringue. Chill 1 hour. Beat whipping cream and the ¼ cup sugar to soft peaks. Fold half of the whipped cream into the remaining chocolate mixture. Carefully spread over the chilled pie. Spread the remaining whipped cream on top. Refrigerate 4 hours or overnight.

Sour Cream Raisin Pie

1 *Pet-Ritz* "Deep Dish" Pie
   Crust Shell
1 cup raisins
   Boiling water
1 cup sugar
¼ cup cornstarch
⅛ teaspoon salt
2¼ cups milk
3 eggs, separated
¼ cup butter *or* margarine
½ cup dairy sour cream
½ teaspoon vanilla
½ teaspoon cream of tartar
6 tablespoons sugar

Thaw pie crust 10 minutes. Prick bottom and sides thoroughly with tines of fork. Bake on preheated cookie sheet in 400° oven for 10 minutes, according to directions on page 6. Remove pie from oven; cool.

To plump raisins, cover with boiling water; let stand 5 minutes. Drain.

In saucepan combine the 1 cup sugar, the cornstarch, and salt. Gradually stir in milk. Cook and stir until thickened and bubbly. Reduce heat; cook and stir 2 minutes more. Remove from heat. Beat egg yolks slightly. Gradually stir 1 cup of the hot mixture into yolks. Return mixture to saucepan; cook and stir 2 minutes more. Remove saucepan from heat. Stir in butter or margarine, and drained raisins. Fold in sour cream. Turn hot cream filling into baked pastry shell. Spread Meringue over hot filling; seal to edge. Bake in 350° oven for 12 to 15 minutes. Cool on wire rack.

Meringue: Beat egg whites, vanilla, and cream of tartar until soft peaks form (tips curl over). Gradually add 6 tablespoons sugar, beating until stiff peaks form (tips stand straight).

Crumb Top Plum Pie

2 pounds fresh red plums, pitted and quartered (about 4 cups)
¼ cup water
1 to 1¼ cups sugar
¼ cup cornstarch
¼ teaspoon salt
1 *Pet-Ritz* "Deep Dish" Pie Crust Shell
⅓ cup all-purpose flour
⅓ cup sugar
½ teaspoon ground cinnamon
¼ teaspoon ground nutmeg
3 tablespoons butter *or* margarine

In medium saucepan combine plums and water. Bring fruit to boiling. Cover and cook over medium heat 3 to 4 minutes. In mixing bowl stir together the 1 cup sugar, the cornstarch, and salt. (Use 1¼ cups sugar if plums are extra tart.) Stir sugar-cornstarch mixture into plums. Cook over low heat, stirring constantly until thickened and bubbly, about 5 minutes. Remove from heat; cool.

Fill frozen pie crust with plum mixture. In small mixing bowl combine flour, the ⅓ cup sugar, the cinnamon, and nutmeg. Cut in butter or margarine until crumbly; sprinkle over plum filling. Bake on preheated cookie sheet in 400° oven for 30 to 35 minutes or until crumb topping is golden brown. Cool on wire rack.

Fresh Spicy Peach Pie

2 *Pet-Ritz* "Deep Dish" Pie Crust Shells
¾ cup sugar
3 tablespoons all-purpose flour
½ teaspoon ground allspice
Dash salt
5 cups sliced, peeled fresh peaches
2 tablespoons butter *or* margarine

Remove pie crusts from freezer. Invert one crust onto waxed paper and let thaw 10 to 15 minutes, according to directions on page 8.

In mixing bowl combine sugar, flour, allspice, and salt. Add to peaches; toss lightly. Pour peach mixture into second crust in pie pan. Dot with butter or margarine. Top with lattice crust, according to directions on page 10.

Bake on preheated cookie sheet in 375° oven for 50 to 55 minutes. Cool on wire rack.

Hawaiian Blueberry Pie

2 *Pet-Ritz* "Deep Dish" Pie Crust Shells
1 jar (12-ounce) pineapple topping
3 tablespoons all-purpose flour
½ teaspoon finely shredded lemon peel
4 cups fresh blueberries, *or* 2 packages (10 ounces each) frozen unsweetened blueberries, thawed
1 tablespoon butter *or* margarine
Pineapple sherbet

Remove pie crusts from freezer. Invert one crust onto waxed paper and let thaw 10 to 15 minutes, according to directions on page 8.

In mixing bowl combine pineapple topping, flour, and lemon peel. Fold in blueberries. Pour berry mixture into second crust in pie pan. Dot with butter or margarine. Top with lattice crust according to directions on page 10.

To prevent overbrowning, cover edge of pie with foil. Bake on preheated cookie sheet in 375° oven for 20 minutes. Remove foil; continue baking 15 to 20 minutes more or until crust is golden. Cool pie on rack before serving. Top individual pie wedges with pineapple sherbet, if desired.

All-American Apple Pie (pictured above)

2 *Pet-Ritz* "Deep Dish" Pie
    Crust Shells
6 cups thinly sliced cooking
    apples (2 pounds)
1 tablespoon lemon juice
    (optional)
1 cup sugar
2 tablespoons all-purpose flour
½ to 1 teaspoon ground cinnamon
    Dash ground nutmeg
1 tablespoon butter *or* margarine
    Sugar (optional)

Remove pie crusts from freezer. Invert one crust onto waxed paper and let thaw 10 to 15 minutes, according to directions on page 8.

If apples lack tartness, sprinkle with 1 tablespoon lemon juice. In mixing bowl combine sugar, flour, cinnamon, and nutmeg. (For a very juicy pie, omit the flour.) Add sugar mixture to the sliced apples, toss to mix. Pour filling into second crust in pie pan; dot with butter or margarine. Moisten edge of crust with a little water. Invert flattened crust on top of filling; tuck edge under and crimp. Cut slits in top crust for steam to escape. Sprinkle some sugar over crust, if desired. Bake on preheated cookie sheet in 375° oven for 45 to 50 minutes. Cool.

Cherry Peach Pie (pictured on back cover)

3 cups peeled, sliced peaches
2 cups pitted tart red cherries
¾ cup sugar
2 *Pet-Ritz* "Deep Dish" Pie
    Crust Shells
¼ cup cornstarch
1 tablespoon lemon juice
2 tablespoons butter *or*
    margarine

In bowl combine peaches, cherries, and sugar. Let stand at room temperature for 1½ hours.

Remove pie crusts from freezer. Invert one crust onto waxed paper and let thaw until flattened, 10 to 15 minutes, according to directions on page 8.

Thoroughly drain fruit, reserving syrup. If necessary, add water to syrup to make 1 cup liquid. In medium saucepan combine cornstarch and the 1 cup fruit syrup. Cook and stir over medium heat until bubbly. Stir in lemon juice. Fold in drained fruit and pour into second crust in pie pan. Dot with butter.

Top with lattice crust, according to directions on page 10. Bake on preheated cookie sheet in 400° oven about 35 minutes. Cool on wire rack.

Apple Apricot Pie

2 *Pet-Ritz* "Deep Dish" Pie
    Crust Shells
⅓ cup granulated sugar
⅓ cup packed brown sugar
3 tablespoons all-purpose flour
¼ teaspoon salt
¼ teaspoon ground cinnamon
1 can (20-ounce) pie-sliced apples
1 tablespoon lemon juice
1 can (30-ounce) apricot halves,
    well drained
1 tablespoon butter *or* margarine
    Milk
    Granulated sugar

Remove pie crusts from freezer. Invert one crust onto waxed paper and let thaw until flattened, 10 to 15 minutes, according to directions on page 8.

In large mixing bowl combine the ⅓ cup granulated sugar, the brown sugar, flour, salt, and cinnamon; add undrained apples. Add lemon juice and mix well. Cut apricot halves in half; fold into apple mixture. Pour filling into second crust in pie pan; dot with butter or margarine. Moisten edge of crust with a little water. Invert flattened crust on top of filling; tuck edge under and crimp. Cut slits in top crust for steam to escape. Brush top crust with milk. Sprinkle with additional granulated sugar. Bake on preheated cookie sheet in 400° oven for 40 minutes. Cool.

Strawberry Rhubarb Pie

1½ cups sugar
3 tablespoons quick-cooking
    tapioca
¼ teaspoon salt
¼ teaspoon ground nutmeg
1 pound rhubarb, cut in ½-inch
    pieces (4 cups)
1 cup sliced fresh strawberries
2 *Pet-Ritz* "Deep Dish" Pie
    Crust Shells
1 tablespoon butter *or* margarine

In large bowl combine sugar, tapioca, salt, and nutmeg. Add rhubarb and strawberries; mix well to coat fruit. Let stand about 20 minutes.

Remove pie crusts from freezer. Invert one crust onto waxed paper and let thaw until flattened, 10 to 15 minutes, according to directions on page 8.

Spoon fruit mixture into second crust in pie pan. Dot with the butter or margarine. Top with lattice crust according to directions on page 10. Bake on preheated cookie sheet in 400° oven for 35 to 40 minutes.

Rhubarb Cherry Pie

2 *Pet-Ritz* "Deep Dish" Pie
   Crust Shells
1 pound rhubarb, cut in ½-inch
   slices (about 4 cups)
1 can (16-ounce) pitted tart red
   cherries, drained
1½ cups sugar
¼ cup quick-cooking tapioca
5 drops red food coloring

Remove pie crusts from freezer. Invert one crust onto waxed paper and let thaw 10 to 15 minutes, according to directions on page 8.

In mixing bowl combine rhubarb, cherries, sugar, tapioca, and food coloring; let stand 15 minutes. Pour filling into second crust in pie pan. Top with lattice crust, according to directions on page 10. Bake on preheated cookie sheet in 400° oven for 40 to 50 minutes. Cool on wire rack.

Cherry Mincemeat Pies

4 *Pet-Ritz* Regular Pie Crust
   Shells
2 cups prepared mincemeat
1 can (21-ounce) cherry pie filling
½ cup orange marmalade
1 tablespoon all-purpose flour
¼ cup chopped *Funsten* Walnuts

Remove pie crust shells from freezer. Invert two crusts onto waxed paper or insert. Let thaw until flattened, 10 to 15 minutes, according to directions on page 8.

In mixing bowl combine mincemeat, cherry pie filling, orange marmalade, flour, and nuts. Divide filling between the two pastry shells in pie pans. Top each with lattice crust, according to directions on page 10. Bake on preheated cookie sheet in 400° oven for 35 to 40 minutes. Cool on wire rack.

Apple Fig Pie

2 *Pet-Ritz* "Deep Dish" Pie
   Crust Shells
1 cup sugar
½ teaspoon salt
½ teaspoon ground cinnamon
¼ teaspoon ground cloves
¼ teaspoon ground nutmeg
4 firm medium apples, peeled,
   cored, and thinly sliced
   (4 cups)
1 cup snipped dried figs
½ cup jellied cranberry sauce
½ teaspoon finely shredded lemon
   peel
¼ cup lemon juice
1 tablespoon butter *or* margarine
1 teaspoon sugar
¼ teaspoon ground cinnamon

Remove pie crusts from freezer. Invert one crust onto waxed paper and let thaw until flattened, 10 to 15 minutes, according to directions on page 8.

In mixing bowl combine the 1 cup sugar, the salt, the ½ teaspoon cinnamon, the cloves, and nutmeg. Add apples, figs, cranberry sauce, lemon peel, and lemon juice; mix well.

Turn apple mixture into second crust in pie pan; dot with butter or margarine. Moisten edge of crust with a little water. Invert flattened crust on top of filling; tuck edge under and crimp. Cut slits in top crust for steam to escape. Brush top crust with *milk*; sprinkle with mixture of the 1 teaspoon sugar and ¼ teaspoon cinnamon. Bake on preheated cookie sheet in 375° oven for 45 to 50 minutes. Cool on wire rack.

Banana Dumplings

2 *Pet-Ritz* "Deep Dish" Pie
   Crust Shells
8 1½-inch pieces peeled, firm
   ripe bananas
2 tablespoons lemon juice
¼ cup sugar
¼ teaspoon ground cinnamon
   Milk

Invert frozen crusts onto waxed paper and let thaw 10 to 15 minutes. Cut each into quarters.

Dip banana pieces in lemon juice. Place a banana piece on each pastry quarter. Combine sugar and cinnamon; sprinkle 1 teaspoon over each banana piece. Moisten edges of pastry. Fold pastry; seal with tines of fork. Brush dumplings with milk; sprinkle each with some of the remaining sugar mixture. Place on cookie sheet. Bake in 425° oven 12 to 15 minutes. Makes 8 dumplings.

Peach Dumplings

2 *Pet-Ritz* "Deep Dish" Pie
   Crust Shells
1 can (29-ounce) peach halves
   Butter *or* margarine
   Ground cinnamon
¼ cup sugar
1 tablespoon cornstarch
   Dash salt
1 teaspoon finely shredded lemon
   peel
1 teaspoon lemon juice
1 tablespoon butter

Remove pie crust shells from freezer. Invert frozen crusts onto waxed paper and let thaw until flattened, 10 to 15 minutes. Invert one flattened crust directly on top of second flattened crust. Roll out to an 18×12-inch rectangle. Cut into six 6-inch squares.

Drain peach halves, reserving 1 cup syrup. Place peach half, cut side down, in center of each square. Dot with a little butter or margarine; sprinkle with cinnamon. Moisten edges of pastry with water. Fold pastry over peach half; pinch together to seal. Place on cookie sheet. Bake in 425° oven for 20 minutes.

In saucepan blend sugar, cornstarch, and salt; gradually add reserved peach syrup. Cook and stir until bubbly. Add lemon peel, lemon juice, and the 1 tablespoon butter. Spoon over dumplings. Makes 6.

Apple Dumplings in Orange Sauce

2 *Pet-Ritz* "Deep Dish" Pie
   Crust Shells
6 medium apples, peeled and
   cored
⅓ cup granulated sugar
1 teaspoon ground cinnamon
2 tablespoons butter *or*
   margarine
½ cup orange marmalade
¼ cup packed brown sugar
1¼ cups orange juice
1 tablespoon lemon juice

Remove pie crust shells from freezer. Invert frozen crusts onto waxed paper and let thaw until flattened, 10 to 15 minutes. Invert one flattened crust directly on top of second flattened crust. Roll out to an 18×12-inch rectangle; cut in six 6-inch squares.

Place apple in center of each square. Combine granulated sugar and the cinnamon; sprinkle about 1 tablespoon over each apple. Dot with butter or margarine. Moisten pastry edges. Fold pastry over apples; pinch to seal. Place in 12×7×2-inch baking dish. In saucepan combine marmalade and brown sugar. Stir in citrus juices; bring to a boil. Pour over dumplings. Bake, uncovered, in 375° oven for 40 to 45 minutes. Makes 6 dumplings.

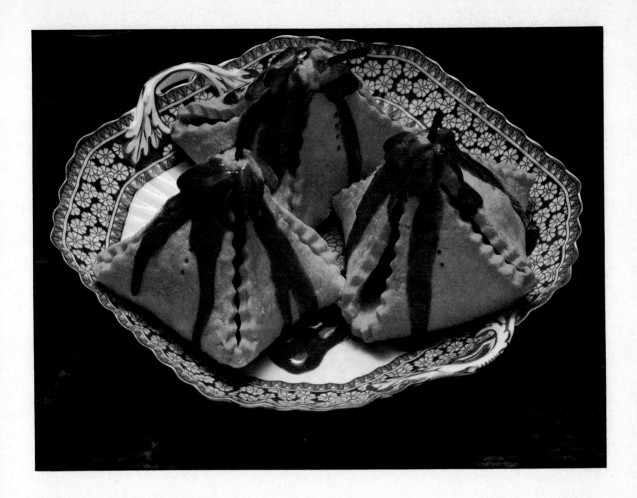

Pear Dumplings Melba (pictured above)

2 *Pet-Ritz* "Deep Dish" Pie
    Crust Shells
4 small pears, peeled and cored
4 tablespoons brown sugar
    Ground cinnamon
    Milk
1 tablespoon cornstarch
1 tablespoon granulated sugar
1 package (10-ounce) frozen red
    raspberries, thawed
3 tablespoons brandy

Remove pie crust shells from freezer. Invert crusts onto waxed paper and let thaw until flattened, 10 to 15 minutes. Invert one flattened crust directly on top of second flattened crust. Roll out to a 14-inch square. Cut into four 7-inch squares.

Place a pear in center of each pastry square. Place 1 tablespoon brown sugar in hollow core of each pear; generously sprinkle cinnamon on top of pears. Moisten edges of pastry with water. Fold corners to center; pinch edges together. Brush with milk. Place dumplings on cookie sheet. Bake in 375° oven for about 40 minutes or till golden.

Meanwhile, in saucepan combine cornstarch and granulated sugar; stir in raspberries. Cook and stir until mixture is thickened and bubbly. Press mixture through sieve to remove seeds; keep warm. To serve, in small saucepan heat brandy. Ignite and pour on top of raspberry sauce. Stir when flame dies; spoon sauce over dumplings. Makes 6 dumplings.

Nutty Banana Turnovers

2 *Pet-Ritz* "Deep Dish" Pie
  Crust Shells
4 medium bananas, peeled
2 tablespoons lemon juice
½ cup chopped *Funsten* Pecans
⅓ cup packed brown sugar
½ teaspoon ground cinnamon
  Milk
  Granulated sugar

Remove pie crust shells from freezer. Invert crusts onto waxed paper or insert and let thaw until flattened, 10 to 15 minutes. Cut each crust into quarters. Slice half a banana onto each pastry quarter. Sprinkle banana with a little lemon juice. Top each with 1 tablespoon of the chopped pecans. Combine brown sugar and cinnamon; sprinkle about 1 tablespoon of the mixture over each square. Fold each pastry quarter in half diagonally; seal edges with tines of fork. Place on cookie sheet. Brush with a little milk and sprinkle with granulated sugar. Bake in 375° oven for 25 to 30 minutes or until golden. Makes 8 turnovers.

Date Turnovers

1 cup (8 ounces) snipped
  pitted dates
½ cup water
¼ cup packed brown sugar
1 tablespoon lemon juice
½ teaspoon vanilla
2 *Pet-Ritz* "Deep Dish" Pie
  Crust Shells
1 beaten egg yolk
1 tablespoon water

In small saucepan combine snipped pitted dates, water, and brown sugar; simmer, uncovered, for 5 minutes, stirring occasionally to keep mixture from sticking. Stir in lemon juice and vanilla. Set filling aside to cool.

Remove pie crust shells from freezer. Invert crusts onto waxed paper and let thaw until flattened, 10 to 15 minutes. Roll each crust to a 14-inch circle. Cut each circle into six 4½-inch rounds Spoon a scant 1 tablespoon date filling on *half* of each circle. Fold over and seal edges with tines of fork. Place on cookie sheet. Brush top with a mixture of egg yolk and the remaining 1 tablespoon water. Bake in 375° oven for 20 to 25 minutes. Makes 12 turnovers.

Mini Mincemeat Turnovers

1 *Pet-Ritz* "Deep Dish" Pie
  Crust Shell
½ cup prepared mincemeat
2 tablespoons shredded sharp
  cheddar cheese
  Milk
  Sugar

Remove pie crust shell from freezer. Invert onto waxed paper or insert and let thaw until flattened, 10 to 15 minutes. Roll crust to a 14-inch circle. Cut into fourteen 3-inch rounds.

Place about 1 teaspoon mincemeat and ¼ teaspoon cheese on *half* of each pastry round. Fold pastry, forming half circles. Seal edges with tines of fork. Brush pastry with milk and sprinkle lightly with sugar. Place on cookie sheet. Bake in 400° oven for 10 to 12 minutes. Cool on rack. Makes 18 turnovers.

Quick Cherry Turnovers

2 *Pet-Ritz* "Deep Dish" Pie
   Crust Shells
1 can (21-ounce) cherry pie filling
¼ cup chopped toasted
   Funsten Almonds
½ cup sifted powdered sugar
1 tablespoon butter *or* margarine, softened
¼ teaspoon vanilla
   Milk

Remove pie crust shells from freezer. Invert crusts onto waxed paper or insert and let thaw until flattened, 10 to 15 minutes (see page 18).

In mixing bowl combine pie filling and almonds; spoon *half* over center of half of each pastry circle, leaving a 1½-inch edge along the outside. Gently fold other half of pastry over filling. Crimp edge to seal. Cut small slits in top. Place on cookie sheet. Bake in 425° oven for 30 minutes or until golden.

Combine powdered sugar, butter or margarine, and vanilla. Stir in enough milk to make of drizzling consistency. Drizzle over warm turnovers. Makes 2.

Tropical Fruit Turnovers

2 *Pet-Ritz* "Deep Dish" Pie
   Crust Shells
½ cup apricot preserves
½ cup flaked coconut
½ cup light raisins
¼ cup chopped pecans
½ cup sifted powdered sugar
¼ teaspoon vanilla
2 to 3 teaspoons milk

Remove pie crust shells from freezer. Invert frozen crusts onto waxed paper and let thaw 10 to 15 minutes. Roll each crust to a 14-inch circle about ⅟₁₆ inch thick. Cut each into six 4½-inch circles.

For filling, combine preserves, coconut, raisins, and pecans. Place 2 tablespoons filling on top of each circle. Fold one side of dough over filling. Seal edges by pressing with tines of fork. Place on cookie sheet; bake in 375° oven for 25 minutes.

Meanwhile, combine powdered sugar, vanilla, and enough milk to make a thin icing. Drizzle icing over warm turnovers. Makes 12 turnovers.

Apple Turnovers

2 *Pet-Ritz* "Deep Dish" Pie
   Crust Shells
¾ pound cooking apples
1 tablespoon lemon juice
⅓ cup sugar
¼ teaspoon ground cinnamon
⅛ teaspoon ground nutmeg
   Dash salt
   Milk
   Sugar
   Ground cinnamon

Remove pie crust shells from freezer. Invert onto waxed paper or insert and let thaw until flattened, 10 to 15 minutes. Cut each crust into quarters.

Meanwhile, peel and core apples; chop apples. Sprinkle apples with lemon juice. Combine the sugar, cinnamon, nutmeg, and salt; toss with apples. Put about ⅓ cup of the apple mixture just off center on a pastry quarter. Fold in half; seal by pressing with tines of fork. Place turnover on cookie sheet. Prick top of pastry for escape of steam. Brush with milk; sprinkle with additional sugar and cinnamon. Repeat with the remaining pastry quarters. Bake in 375° oven for 30 to 35 minutes, or until crust is golden. Cool on wire rack. Makes 8.

Dazzling desserts to dwell on

M ound fluffy chiffons or ice
cream fillings into a baked
pastry shell or graham cracker
crust—and you have an easy, but
impressive dessert. In one easy
step, turn the pastry shell into a
pizza-size pie crust and assemble
a decorative flan. Or, use the
graham cracker shell for a baked
cheesecake, topped with a showy
fruit glaze. How about serving the
Strawberry Chiffon Pie shown
here to make your next special
occasion extra special? The
recipe is on page 82. On the
following pages, you'll find these
and many other desserts to dazzle
your guests.

Banana Split Pie

1 *Pet-Ritz* "Deep Dish" Pie
    Crust Shell
2 medium bananas
1 tablespoon lemon juice
1 quart strawberry ice cream
1 cup *Pet Whip* Non-Dairy
    Whipped Topping, thawed
⅓ cup maraschino cherries (12)
2 tablespoons chopped *Funsten*
    Walnuts
½ cup tiny marshmallows
¼ cup semisweet chocolate pieces
2 tablespoons milk

Thaw pie crust 10 minutes. Prick bottom and sides thoroughly with tines of fork. Bake on preheated cookie sheet in 400° oven for 10 minutes (see page 6). Remove crust from oven; cool.

Thinly slice bananas and sprinkle with lemon juice. Arrange the bananas on bottom of pie crust. In mixing bowl soften strawberry ice cream using a wooden spoon to stir and press against side of bowl. Soften until just pliable. Using a metal spatula, spread ice cream over the sliced bananas in pie crust.

Spread the *Pet Whip* over the frozen ice cream layer in pie crust. Top with cherries; sprinkle with nuts. Return pie to freezer; freeze several hours.

Meanwhile, in saucepan combine marshmallows, chocolate, and milk. Cook over low heat, stirring constantly, until marshmallows and chocolate melt.

Let pie stand about 15 minutes at room temperature before serving. Drizzle with sauce.

Strawberry Chiffon Pie (pictured on pages 80–81)

1 *Pet-Ritz* "Deep Dish" Pie
    Crust Shell
2½ cups fresh strawberries
¼ cup sugar
1 tablespoon lemon juice
¼ cup sugar
1 envelope unflavored gelatin
¾ cup water
2 egg whites
¼ cup sugar
½ cup whipping cream

Thaw crust 10 minutes. Prick pie crust shell with fork. Bake on preheated cookie sheet in a 400° oven for 10 minutes, according to directions on page 6. Cool.

Reserve a few strawberries for garnish; set aside. Crush enough of the remaining strawberries to measure 1¼ cups crushed berries. Stir in ¼ cup, sugar and the lemon juice; let stand 30 minutes.

Meanwhile, in small saucepan stir together ¼ cup sugar and gelatin. Stir in water; heat and stir until sugar and gelatin dissolve. Cool; stir into strawberry mixture. Chill to the consistency of corn syrup, stirring occasionally. Remove from refrigerator (gelatin mixture will continue to set).

Immediately begin beating egg whites until soft peaks form. Gradually add ¼ cup sugar, beating until stiff peaks form. When gelatin is partially set fold in egg whites.

Beat whipping cream until soft peaks form. Fold whipped cream into strawberry mixture. Chill until mixture mounds when spooned. Pile mixture into baked pastry shell. Chill pie 8 hours or until firm. Garnish with reserved strawberries and additional whipped cream, if desired.

Strawberry Sunshine Pie (pictured above)

1 *Pet-Ritz* "Deep Dish" Pie
  Crust Shell
1 pint lemon *or* orange sherbet
2 cups fresh strawberries, sliced
1 tablespoon sugar
3 egg whites
½ teaspoon vanilla
¼ teaspoon cream of tartar
⅓ cup sugar

Thaw pie crust 10 minutes. Prick bottom and sides thoroughly with tines of fork. Bake on preheated cookie sheet in 400° oven for 10 minutes, according to directions on page 6. Remove pie crust from oven; cool.

In mixing bowl soften sherbet using a wooden spoon to stir and press against side of bowl. Soften until just pliable. Using a metal spatula, spread sherbet in pie crust. Freeze several hours or overnight until firm.

Combine strawberries and the 1 tablespoon sugar; set aside. In mixer bowl prepare meringue by beating egg whites, vanilla, and cream of tartar until soft peaks form (tips curl over). Gradually add ⅓ cup sugar, beating to stiff peaks (tips stand straight). Working quickly, arrange strawberry-sugar mixture over sherbet layer in pastry shell. Spread meringue over berries, carefully sealing to edge of pastry. Bake on cookie sheet in 475° oven for 3 to 5 minutes, or until golden. Slice pie and serve immediately.

Mile High Ice Cream Pie

1 *Pet-Ritz* "Deep Dish" Pie
    Crust Shell
1 pint chocolate ice cream,
    softened
1 pint strawberry ice cream,
    softened
4 egg whites
½ teaspoon vanilla
¼ teaspoon cream of tartar
½ cup sugar
4 1-ounce squares unsweetened
    chocolate, cut-up
¾ cup water
1 cup sugar
    Dash salt
6 tablespoons butter
1 teaspoon vanilla

Thaw pie crust 10 minutes. Prick. Bake on preheated cookie sheet in 400° oven for 10 minutes (see page 6). Remove from oven; cool. Spread chocolate ice cream in crust; top with strawberry ice cream; freeze.

Beat egg whites with the ½ teaspoon vanilla and cream of tartar until soft peaks form. Gradually add ½ cup sugar, beating until stiff peaks form. Spread meringue over ice cream, sealing to edge of crust. Bake in 475° oven 2 to 3 minutes or until meringue is lightly browned. Freeze several hours. Cut in wedges and drizzle with Chocolate Sauce.

Chocolate Sauce: Heat chocolate and water until smooth. Stir in the 1 cup sugar and the salt. Simmer 5 minutes. Remove from heat; blend in butter and 1 teaspoon vanilla.

Frozen Yogurt Pie (pictured on pages 4-5)

½ cup boiling water
1 package (7.2-ounce) fluffy white
    frosting mix
2 cartons (8 ounces each) rasp-
    berry yogurt (2 cups)
1 *Pet-Ritz* Graham Cracker
    Crust
    Pet Whip Non-Dairy Whipped
    Topping, thawed

In small mixer bowl pour boiling water over frosting mix; beat at high speed on electric mixer 5 minutes or until stiff peaks form. Carefully fold in yogurt; pour into graham cracker crust. Freeze several hours or overnight. Remove from freezer 10 to 15 minutes before serving. Garnish top of pie with *Pet Whip* and mint sprig, if desired.

Pineapple Fluff Pie

1 package (3¼- or 3½-ounce)
    vanilla tapioca pudding mix
1 package (3-ounce) lemon-
    flavored gelatin
1¼ cups milk
½ of a 6-ounce can frozen pine-
    apple juice concentrate
    (⅓ cup)
2 cups *Pet Whip* Non-Dairy
    Whipped Topping, thawed
1 can (8¼-ounce) crushed pineapple,
    well drained
2 *Pet-Ritz* Graham Cracker Crusts

In saucepan combine pudding mix and gelatin. Stir in milk. Cook and stir until thickened and bubbly (mixture may appear curdled during cooking). Remove from heat. Stir in pineapple juice concentrate. Chill mixture until partially set (the consistency of unbeaten egg whites), stirring occasionally.

Fold *Pet Whip* into gelatin mixture. Fold in well drained crushed pineapple. Chill until mixture mounds when spooned. Divide mixture between graham cracker crusts; chill several hours or overnight until set.

Date Nut Ice Cream Pie

1 *Pet-Ritz* "Deep Dish" Pie
    Crust Shell
1 quart vanilla ice cream
1⅓ cups snipped pitted dates
1 tablespoon sugar
1 tablespoon lemon juice
1 teaspoon vanilla
¼ cup chopped *Funsten* Walnuts
2 cups *Pet Whip* Non-Dairy
    Whipped Topping, thawed

Thaw pie crust 10 minutes. Prick bottom and sides thoroughly with tines of fork. Bake on preheated cookie sheet in 400° oven for 10 minutes. Remove from oven; cool. Stir ice cream to soften; spread in bottom of pie crust. Freeze until firm. In saucepan combine dates, ¾ cup *water*, and sugar; cook, covered until dates are softened, about 5 minutes. Stir in lemon juice and vanilla; cool. Spread *half* of date mixture over ice cream in pie crust. Fold remaining date mixture and walnuts into *Pet Whip*; spoon over date layer. Freeze.

Lemon Frost Pie

2 egg whites
⅔ cup sugar
2 teaspoons finely shredded
    lemon peel
¼ cup lemon juice
5 drops yellow food coloring
1 cup whipping cream, whipped
1 *Pet-Ritz* Graham Cracker
    Crust
1 recipe Blueberry Sauce

Combine egg whites, the ⅔ cup sugar, the lemon peel and juice, and food coloring; beat to stiff peaks. Fold whipped cream into lemon mixture. Turn into graham cracker crust. Chill or freeze.

Serve with *Blueberry Sauce*: Combine ⅔ cup *sugar*, 1 tablespoon *cornstarch*, and dash *salt*. Add ⅔ cup *water*. Cook and stir until thickened and bubbly; cook 2 minutes more. Add 2 cups *fresh blueberries*; return to boiling. Chill.

Candy Bar Pie

1 teaspoon instant coffee crystals
1 milk chocolate candy bar with
    almonds (7½-ounce), broken
1 container *Pet Whip* Non-Dairy
    Whipped Topping, thawed
1 *Pet-Ritz* Graham Cracker
    Crust

In small saucepan dissolve coffee crystals in 2 tablespoons *water*; add chocolate bar. Stir chocolate mixture over low heat until melted; cool. Fold in *Pet Whip*; spoon into graham cracker crust. Chill in freezer several hours or overnight (it will not freeze solid).

Hot Fudge Peanut Pie

3 eggs
1 cup chocolate syrup
½ teaspoon vanilla
½ cup packed brown sugar
1¼ cups peanuts, chopped
1 *Pet-Ritz* Graham Cracker
    Crust
    Coffee ice cream

In bowl beat eggs slightly. Add chocolate syrup and vanilla. Blend in brown sugar; and *1 cup* of the nuts. Pour into graham cracker crust. Bake in 350° oven for 40 minutes. Remove from oven; chill. Top each wedge with ice cream and sprinkle with some of the remaining peanuts.

Neapolitan Ice Cream Pie

1 pint vanilla ice cream
1 cup dairy sour cream
3 tablespoons light rum
1 *Pet-Ritz* Graham Cracker
    Crust
1 pint chocolate ice cream
1 pint strawberry ice cream
½ square (½ ounce) semisweet
    chocolate
1 teaspoon butter *or* margarine

In mixing bowl soften vanilla ice cream using a wooden spoon to stir and press against side of bowl. Combine sour cream and light rum; stir into softened ice cream. Freeze ice cream mixture until nearly firm. Using metal spatula, spread the ice cream in crust. Arrange scoops of chocolate and strawberry ice cream over vanilla ice cream layer. Freeze several hours or overnight.

Before serving, combine semisweet chocolate and butter; heat over low heat until melted, stirring constantly. Remove pie from the freezer. Drizzle the warm chocolate mixture over pie. Serve immediately.

Peach Parfait Pie

3½ cups peeled, sliced fresh
    peaches
¼ cup sugar
1 package (3-ounce) lemon-
    flavored gelatin
1 pint vanilla ice cream
2 *Pet-Ritz* Graham Cracker
    Crusts
  Pet Whip Non-Dairy Whipped
    Topping, thawed
  Ground nutmeg

In mixing bowl combine peaches and sugar; let stand about 15 minutes. Drain peaches, reserving the syrup and 10 peach slices. Add enough water to the syrup to measure 1 cup liquid. Bring fruit liquid to boiling; remove from heat. Add gelatin; stir until dissolved. Pour gelatin mixture into large mixing bowl. Add ice cream by spoonfuls, stirring until melted. Chill until mixture mounds when spooned. Fold in sliced peaches. Divide mixture between graham cracker crusts. Chill pies several hours or overnight until set. Arrange the reserved peach slices spoke-fashion on top of pies. Garnish with *Pet Whip* and sprinkle with nutmeg.

Blueberry Yogurt Chiffon Pie

¼ cup sugar
1 envelope unflavored gelatin
½ teaspoon salt
¼ cup water
2 slightly beaten egg yolks
1 cup cream-style cottage cheese
1 carton (8-ounce) blueberry
    yogurt (1 cup)
2 egg whites
¼ cup sugar
1 *Pet-Ritz* Graham Cracker
    Crust

In saucepan combine the first ¼ cup sugar, the gelatin, and salt; stir in water and egg yolks. Cook and stir until the mixture is slightly thickened; cool.

Sieve cottage cheese; stir in gelatin mixture. Add yogurt; beat until blended. Immediately beat egg whites until soft peaks form (tips curl over). Gradually add the remaining ¼ cup sugar, beating until stiff peaks form (tips stand straight). Fold stiff-beaten egg whites into the gelatin mixture. Chill until mixture mounds when spooned. Turn into graham cracker crust. Chill several hours or overnight until set.

Lime Daiquiri Pie

1 *Pet-Ritz* "Deep Dish" Pie
   Crust Shell
⅔ cup sugar
1 envelope unflavored gelatin
¼ teaspoon salt
⅓ cup lime juice
⅓ cup water
3 slightly beaten egg yolks
½ teaspoon finely shredded lime
   peel
6 to 8 drops green food coloring
   (optional)
¼ cup light rum
3 egg whites
⅓ cup sugar

Thaw pie crust 10 minutes. Prick bottom and sides thoroughly with tines of fork. Bake on preheated cookie sheet in 400° oven for 10 minutes, according to directions on page 6. Remove pie from oven; cool.

Combine the ⅔ cup sugar, the gelatin, and salt. Stir in lime juice, water, and egg yolks. Cook and stir over low heat until mixture thickens slightly. Remove from heat. Stir in lime peel; add food coloring, if desired. Cool slightly; stir in rum. Chill to the consistency of corn syrup, stirring occasionally. Immediately beat egg whites until soft peaks form. Gradually add the ⅓ cup sugar, beating to stiff peaks. When gelatin is partially set, fold in egg whites. Chill until mixture mounds. Turn into pie crust. Chill several hours.

Caramel Pecan Pie

28 vanilla caramels (8 ounces)
1¼ cups milk
1 envelope unflavored gelatin
¼ cup cold water
1 teaspoon vanilla
⅛ teaspoon salt
1 cup *Pet Whip* Non-Dairy
   Whipped Topping, thawed
½ cup chopped *Funsten* Pecans
1 *Pet-Ritz* Graham Cracker
   Crust

Heat and stir vanilla caramels and milk over low heat for 20 minutes or until caramels are melted. Meanwhile, soften gelatin in cold water. Add gelatin to caramel mixture; stir until dissolved. Stir in vanilla and salt. Chill mixture to the consistency of corn syrup, stirring occasionally. (Watch gelatin mixture closely; caramels make the mixture set up quickly.)

When gelatin is partially set, fold in *Pet Whip* and nuts. Chill until mixture mounds when spooned. Turn into crust. Chill several hours or overnight.

Malt Shop Pie

1 pint vanilla ice cream
½ cup crushed malted milk balls
1 tablespoon milk
1 *Pet-Ritz* Graham Cracker
   Crust
3 tablespoons instant chocolate-
   flavored malted milk powder
3 tablespoons marshmallow
   topping
1 tablespoon milk
1 cup *Pet Whip* Non-Dairy
   Whipped Topping, thawed

In a chilled medium bowl stir ice cream to soften; blend in the ½ cup crushed malted milk balls and the first 1 tablespoon milk. Spread in graham cracker crust; freeze while preparing top layer. In medium bowl blend malted milk powder, marshmallow topping, and remaining milk. Fold in *Pet Whip*. Spread mixture over layer in graham cracker crust. Freeze until firm, several hours or overnight. Sprinkle with additional crushed malted milk balls, if desired.

Mixed Fruit Flan

1 envelope unflavored gelatin
¼ cup sugar
2 cups milk
3 slightly beaten eggs
1 teaspoon vanilla
½ cup apricot jam
4 cups banana slices, orange segments, pineapple slices, peach slices, apricot halves, seeded grapes, *or* pitted cherries

Prepare 12-inch flan crust according to directions on page 18. Bake in a 400° oven for 12 to 15 minutes.

In the saucepan combine gelatin and sugar. Stir in milk; bring mixture to a boil, stirring constantly. Gradually stir half of the hot mixture into the beaten eggs. Return egg mixture to saucepan; cook and stir for ½ minute. Remove from heat; add vanilla. Cover surface with clear plastic wrap; chill until partially set (consistency of unbeaten egg whites). Pour partially set custard over crust. In small saucepan heat jam over low heat till melted. Arrange choice of fruits over custard; brush with melted jam. Chill 1 to 2 hours. Cut into wedges to serve. Makes 10 servings.

Cottage Cheese Pie

1 *Pet-Ritz* "Deep Dish" Pie Crust Shell
2 beaten egg yolks
1½ cups (12 ounces) cream-style cottage cheese
⅔ cup sugar
2 tablespoons butter *or* margarine, melted
½ cup milk
2 egg whites

Prebake *unpricked* pie crust on preheated cookie sheet in 450° oven for 6 minutes, according to directions on page 6. Remove pie crust from oven. Reduce oven temperature to 350°.

Beat together egg yolks, cottage cheese, sugar, and melted butter until nearly smooth. Stir in milk. Beat egg whites until stiff peaks form (tips stand straight). Fold egg whites into cottage cheese mixture. Pour into partially baked pastry shell. Bake on preheated cookie sheet in 350° oven 25 to 30 minutes, or until a knife inserted just off center comes out clean. Chill several hours before serving.

Peach Cheesecake Pie

1 *Pet-Ritz* "Deep Dish" Pie Crust Shell
1 package (8-ounce) cream cheese, softened
1 cup sifted powdered sugar
1 teaspoon vanilla
1½ cups *Pet-Whip* Non-Dairy Whipped Topping, thawed
1 can (21-ounce) peach pie filling, chilled

Thaw pie crust 10 minutes. Prick bottom and sides thoroughly with tines of fork. Bake on preheated cookie sheet in 400° oven for 10 minutes, according to directions on page 6. Remove pie crust from oven; cool on wire rack.

Beat together cream cheese, sugar, and vanilla until smooth. Fold in *Pet Whip*. Spoon into pie crust. Spoon pie filling over cheese mixture. Chill until set.

Italian Orange Flan (pictured above)

1 *Pet-Ritz* "Deep Dish" Pie
   Crust Shell
⅓ cup sugar
2 tablespoons cornstarch
¼ teaspoon salt
1¼ cups milk
3 beaten egg yolks
3 tablespoons brandy
3 oranges, peeled and sectioned
2 bananas, sliced
½ cup orange marmalade

Transfer frozen pie shell to a 10-inch flan pan; thaw 10 minutes. Press to fit pastry to pan, according to directions on page 6. Crimp edge. Prick bottom. Bake in 400° oven for 10 minutes. Cool in pan. Litt crust from pan onto platter.

In saucepan combine sugar, cornstarch, and salt; add milk. Cook and stir until bubbly. Cook 2 minutes more. Remove from heat. Gradually stir *half* of hot mixture into yolks; return all to hot mixture. Cook and stir just until bubbly; remove from heat; stir in brandy. Cover surface with clear plastic wrap; cool 30 minutes. Spread custard in shell. Chill. About 1 hour before serving, arrange fruit over custard. Melt marmalade; spoon over fruit. Chill. Makes 8 to 10 servings.

Fruit and Nut Flan

2 *Pet-Ritz* "Deep Dish" Pie
  Crust Shells
½ cup granulated sugar
4 teaspoons cornstarch
¼ teaspoon ground cinnamon
¾ cup orange juice
5 large oranges, pared and
  sectioned
¼ cup chopped *Funsten* Pecans
¼ cup shredded coconut
½ cup dairy sour cream
2 tablespoons powdered sugar

Prepare 12-inch flan crust, according to directions on page 18. Bake in 450° oven for 6 minutes. Meanwhile, in 1-quart saucepan, combine granulated sugar, cornstarch, and cinnamon; stir in orange juice. Cook and stir until thickened and bubbly. Spread over partially baked crust; arrange orange sections over glaze. Sprinkle with pecans and coconut. Bake in 375° oven 15 to 20 minutes more. Combine sour cream and powdered sugar; serve with warm flan slices. Makes 10 servings.

Cherry Cheese Flan

2 *Pet-Ritz* "Deep Dish" Pie
  Crust Shells
1 package (8-ounce) cream
  cheese, softened
½ cup sugar
2 eggs
⅓ cup chopped walnuts
1 teaspoon vanilla
2 cans (21 ounces each) cherry
  pie filling

Prepare 12-inch flan crust, according to directions on page 18. Bake in 450° oven for 6 minutes. Blend cream cheese and sugar; add eggs and beat well. Add nuts and vanilla. Pour into partially baked crust and bake in 350° oven for 10 minutes more; cool.

Spread cherry pie filling over cheese layer. Chill. Top chilled pie with dollops of whipped cream cheese or whipped cream. To serve, cut in wedges. Makes 10 servings.

Strawberry Flan

2 *Pet-Ritz* "Deep Dish" Pie
  Crust Shells
1 package (2¼-ounce) no-bake
  custard-flavored dessert mix
2 cups milk
1 package (8-ounce) cream
  cheese, cubed
½ teaspoon vanilla
2 cups fresh strawberries, halved
1 can (8-ounce) sliced peaches,
  drained
1 small banana, sliced
2 tablespoons cornstarch
2 tablespoons sugar
⅔ cup orange juice
½ cup red currant jelly

Prepare 12-inch flan crust, according to directions on page 18. Bake in 400° oven for 12 to 15 minutes. In saucepan add custard mix to milk. Cook and stir over medium heat until mixture comes to rolling boil; cook 3 minutes more. Remove from heat. Stir in cream cheese and vanilla, beating smooth with rotary beater. Cool 10 minutes, stirring occasionally. Spoon onto pastry. Chill until nearly firm. Arrange halved strawberries around edge, sliced peaches in a spoke pattern in the middle, and banana slices in the center.

In small saucepan combine the cornstarch, sugar, and ¼ teaspoon ground *mace*. Stir in orange juice; add jelly. Cook and stir until mixture thickens and bubbles; cook 2 minutes more. Cool slightly. Spoon over arranged fruit. Chill well. Makes 10 servings.

Cheesecake Pecan Pie

1 package (8-ounce) cream cheese
1 egg
⅓ cup sugar
½ teaspoon vanilla
1 *Pet-Ritz* "Deep Dish" Pie
    Crust Shell
1 cup *Funsten* Pecan Halves
2 slightly beaten eggs
¼ cup sugar
⅔ cup dark corn syrup
¼ teaspoon maple flavoring
¼ teaspoon vanilla

In small mixer bowl combine softened cream cheese, the egg, and ⅓ cup sugar, and the ½ teaspoon vanilla. Beat until mixture is light and fluffy. Spread over bottom of the pie crust. Arrange pecan halves on top of the whipped cream cheese mixture.

In bowl combine the 2 eggs, the ¼ cup sugar, the corn syrup, maple flavoring, and vanilla; mix well. Carefully pour over pecans. Bake on a preheated cookie sheet in 375° oven 40 to 45 minutes or until done. Makes 6 to 8 servings.

Blueberry Cheesecake Pie

1½ cups cream-style cottage
    cheese, well-drained
3 eggs
½ cup sugar
2 tablespoons all-purpose flour
1 tablespoon lemon juice
1 teaspoon vanilla
1 small can (5.33 fl. oz.) Pet
    Evaporated Milk (⅔ cup)
2 *Pet-Ritz* Graham Cracker
    Crusts
1 can (21-ounce) blueberry pie
    filling, chilled

In mixing bowl beat drained cottage cheese with electric mixer or rotary beater about 5 minutes or until creamy and nearly smooth. Add eggs, sugar, flour, lemon juice, and vanilla; mix well to thoroughly combine. Stir in evaporated milk.

Divide filling between graham cracker crusts. Bake in 350° oven for 25 to 30 minutes or until knife inserted off center comes out clean. Cool pies on rack; chill thoroughly. Spread chilled blueberry pie filling over pies before serving.

Banana Spice Cheesecake

1 package (8-ounce) cream
    cheese, softened
2 tablespoons sugar
2 eggs, separated
½ cup mashed ripe banana
⅔ cup *sweetened condensed* milk
1 teaspoon vanilla
1 tablespoon all-purpose flour
⅛ teaspoon salt
⅛ teaspoon ground ginger
⅛ teaspoon ground cinnamon
1 *Pet-Ritz* Graham Cracker
    Crust
½ cup dairy sour cream

In large mixer bowl cream together cream cheese and sugar. Add egg yolks; beat well. Blend in banana, then milk and vanilla. Stir together flour, salt, and spices; stir into cream cheese mixture. Beat egg whites to stiff peaks; fold into cream cheese mixture. Spoon into graham cracker crust. Bake in 350° oven for 25 minutes or until knife inserted off center comes out clean.

Meanwhile, combine sour cream, 1 tablespoon *sugar*, and ½ teaspoon *vanilla*; spread over hot cheesecake. Cool. Chill. Top with banana slices, if desired. Makes 6 to 8 servings.

Strawberry Cheesecake Pie (pictured on front cover)

1 package (10½- or 11-ounce)
  cheesecake mix
⅓ cup chopped *Funsten* Almonds,
  toasted
2 *Pet-Ritz* Graham Cracker
  Crusts
1 cup sugar
2 tablespoons cornstarch
1 quart strawberries
  Water
1 package (3-ounce) strawberry-
  flavored gelatin
1 tablespoon butter *or* margarine
1 tablespoon lemon juice

Prepare cheesecake mix according to package directions; stir in almonds. (Set aside graham cracker crumbs for another use.) Divide filling between graham cracker crusts; chill 1 hour.

Meanwhile, in saucepan combine sugar and cornstarch. Mash 1 cup of the strawberries; add water to make 2 cups. Stir into sugar mixture. Cook and stir until mixture thickens and bubbles; cook 2 minutes more. Remove from heat; strain. Add gelatin, butter or margarine and lemon juice; stir until gelatin dissolves. Chill until partially set.

Spoon 1½ cups of the gelatin mixture over cheesecake mixture. Arrange remaining strawberries over pies. Carefully spoon remaining gelatin over berries. Chill until set.

Speedy Cheesecake Pie

1 package (8-ounce) cream
  cheese, softened
½ cup sugar
1 tablespoon lemon juice
½ teaspoon vanilla
2 eggs
1 *Pet-Ritz* Graham Cracker
  Crust
1 cup dairy sour cream
2 tablespoons sugar
½ teaspoon vanilla
1 package (10-ounce) frozen
  sliced strawberries, thawed

Beat cream cheese until fluffy. Gradually blend in the ½ cup sugar, lemon juice, ½ teaspoon vanilla, and a dash *salt*. Add eggs, one at a time, beating well after each.

Pour filling into graham cracker crust. Bake in 325° oven until set, 25 to 30 minutes.

Combine sour cream, 2 tablespoons sugar, and ½ teaspoon vanilla. Spoon over top of pie. Bake 10 minutes longer. Cool. Chill several hours. Cut in wedges. Spoon strawberries over individual servings.

Cheesecake Fruit Cocktail Pie

2 cups tiny marshmallows *or* 20
  large marshmallows
2 tablespoons milk
1 cup dairy sour cream
1 package (3-ounce) cream
  cheese, softened
1 teaspoon vanilla
1 can (17-ounce) fruit cocktail,
  drained
2 *Pet-Ritz* Graham Cracker
  Crusts

In heavy saucepan heat marshmallows and milk over low heat until marshmallows are melted, stirring frequently. Cool about 10 minutes. In mixer bowl beat sour cream, softened cream cheese, vanilla, and a dash *salt* with electric mixer until smooth. Stir in marshmallow mixture and drained fruit cocktail. Spoon into graham cracker crusts. Chill several hours or overnight until set.

Mandarin Banana Cheese Pie

2½ cups milk
1 package (4½-ounce) no-bake
   custard mix
1 package (8-ounce) cream
   cheese, cubed
¾ teaspoon finely shredded
   orange peel
2 large bananas, sliced
2 *Pet-Ritz* Graham Cracker
   Crusts
⅔ cup orange juice
2 teaspoons cornstarch
1 can (11-ounce) mandarin orange sections, drained

In saucepan combine milk and custard mix. Stir in cubed cream cheese and orange peel. Cook until mixture is thickened and bubbly, stirring constantly. Remove from heat; beat with rotary beater until smooth. Cool 15 minutes. Arrange half the banana slices in the bottom of each graham cracker crust. Carefully pour cheese mixture over banana layer in each crust. Chill several hours. Serve with Orange Sauce.

Orange Sauce: In saucepan combine orange juice and cornstarch. Cook and stir until thickened and bubbly. Cool slightly; stir in orange sections. Serve sauce warm or chilled.

Pear Strawberry Flan

1 *Pet-Ritz* "Deep Dish" Pie
   Crust Shell
1 can (29-ounce) pear halves
1 package (10-ounce) frozen
   strawberries, thawed
2 tablespoons cornstarch
¼ cup currant jelly
   Pet Whip Non-Dairy Whipped
   Topping, thawed

Thaw pie crust 10 minutes. Prick bottom and sides thoroughly with tines of fork. Bake on preheated cookie sheet in 400° oven for 10 minutes, according to directions on page 6. Remove pie crust from oven; cool.

Drain pears and strawberries, reserving syrups. Slice pears; arrange in baked pastry shell with berries. Measure reserved strawberry syrup; add pear syrup to equal 1 cup liquid. In saucepan stir syrup mixture into cornstarch; add currant jelly. Cook and stir over medium-high heat until mixture thickens and bubbles. Remove from heat. Cover surface of thickened syrup mixture with clear plastic wrap. Cool 30 minutes. Spoon cooled glaze over fruit in pastry shell. Top with *Pet Whip*.

Peach Pineapple Cheesecake Pie

1 *Pet-Ritz* "Deep Dish" Pie
   Crust Shell
1 can (21-ounce) peach pie filling
1 can (8¼-ounce) crushed
   pineapple, drained
1 cup dairy sour cream
1 package (3-ounce) cream
   cheese, softened
2 slightly beaten eggs
⅓ cup sugar

Prebake *unpricked* pie crust shell on preheated cookie sheet in 450° oven for 6 minutes, according to directions on page 6. Remove pie crust from oven. Reduce oven temperature to 375°.

In mixing bowl combine pie filling and pineapple; turn into baked pastry shell. In small mixer bowl beat together sour cream and cream cheese until fluffy; add eggs and sugar, beating until smooth. Pour cheese mixture over peach-pineapple filling. Bake in 375° oven 30 minutes. Cool on wire rack.

INDEX

D-L

M-P

INDEX Continued

Pie crust basics